SOPHOCLES'

OEDIPUS THE KING

AND

OEDIPUS AT COLONUS

CHARLES R. WALKER graduated from Yale, where he majored in Greek and was chairman of the Yale Literary Magazine. During World War I he was commissioned a second lieutenant in the heavy artillery, an experience that resulted in a lifelong interest in men and technology and led him to go to work in the early twenties as a laborer in steel and copper mills. His subsequent career has continued to revolve around this somewhat unconventional duality–literature and Greek translation on the one hand, and industry and technology on the other. From 1945 to 1962 he was Director of the Technology Project at Yale University. His published works include: *Steel: The Diary of a Furnace Worker; Bread and Fire,* a novel; *Our Gods Are Not Born,* a book of short stories; *Steeltown,* a study of industrial and technological change; *Toward the Automatic Factory; The Man on the Assembly Line* (with Robert H. Guest); *Technology and Civilization;* and *Iphigenia in Aulis,* in the Grene-Lattimore edition of the complete Greek tragedies, published by the University of Chicago Press. In 1957 Mr. Walker received a grant from the Bollingen Foundation which enabled him to travel in Greece and complete the translations and essays that comprise this volume.

SOPHOCLES'

Oedipus the King

AND

Oedipus at Colonus

A NEW TRANSLATION FOR

MODERN READERS AND THEATERGOERS BY

Charles R. Walker

1966

Anchor Books

DOUBLEDAY & COMPANY, INC.

GARDEN CITY, NEW YORK

PA
4414
A2W27

ACKNOWLEDGMENTS

I would like to express my gratitude:

To Bernard Knox for his understanding criticism and encouragement.

To Alexis Minotis for his many unforgettable portrayals of Oedipus in the modern theater.

To my first teachers of Greek at the high school in Concord, New Hampshire, and at Phillips Exeter Academy.

To the Bollingen Foundation for its generous financial assistance.

Caution: the translation of these two plays is the sole property of the translator and is protected by copyright. It may not be acted by professionals or amateurs without formal permission. All rights, including professional, amateur, stock, radio, television broadcasting, motion pictures, recitation, lecturing, public reading, and copying are reserved. All inquiries should be addressed to the translator in care of Doubleday & Company, Inc., 277 Park Avenue, New York, N.Y. 10017.

LIBRARY OF CONGRESS CATALOG CARD NUMBER 66–11183
COPYRIGHT © 1966 BY CHARLES R. WALKER
ALL RIGHTS RESERVED
PRINTED IN THE UNITED STATES OF AMERICA
FIRST EDITION

To

Adelaide George Walker

with gratitude

39100

CONTENTS

THE RETURN OF OEDIPUS

If it were possible to count all the performances of *Oedipus the King* since its first showing at the theater of Dionysus on the side of the Acropolis in 429 B.C., it would undoubtedly emerge as the most continuously produced play in dramatic history. As to its reputation as a masterpiece—not to mention the ink spent to explain it—it competes with *Hamlet.* But something quite new has happened to *Oedipus,* as theater, since the Second World War. This ancient story of incest and murder is now known, because of Freud and the "Oedipus complex," to millions of men and women in the modern world. Familiarity with the outline of the story, however, is, at most, only a contributory cause to the triumphal re-entry of Sophocles' play into the theaters of Europe, England, and the United States. There are many causes and long before the present wave of neo-Hellenism—or, as a friend, after a trip to Athens, has called it, "*neon*-Hellenism"—I have been convinced that *Oedipus* and other Greek plays have begun to speak to the modern world with the authority of living theater. How and why has this happened?

Oedipus the King, aside from its subtleties of poetry and theme, is, of course, superb theater. It has the kind of hard, bony structure that can withstand almost any degree of bad direction and acting. But there are elements other than sheer theatrical effectiveness which account for its power. These relate to the mythical material out of which Sophocles and other ancient dramatists constructed their plays, material which has continued to attract writers up to the present day.

Here, however, we shall be concerned chiefly with *Oedipus* as theater, past and present. First examine the record: The great period of classical drama lasted from sometime before Thespis won his first prize, in 534 B.C., to 401 B.C., when the last of Sophocles' plays, *Oedipus at Colonus,* was performed five years after the poet's death. But the Oedipus story ante dates Sophocles' day by many centuries—perhaps millennia Our first written record comes from Homer in the eighth cen tury B.C. By the time Greek tragedies began to be performe regularly in Athens, in the fifth century, everyone knew th story, for not only had all the great dramatists used it, but i had been the subject of two epic poems (now lost)—the *Oedi podia* and the *Thebaid* (which concerned Oedipus' sons) Aeschylus wrote a trilogy on Laius (father of Oedipus), o Oedipus himself, and on his two sons (Eteocles and Polynices) Only the last of these, *Seven Against Thebes,* is extant. Euri pides wrote an *Oedipus,* which is lost, but there survives hi very long play, *The Phoenician Women,* which deals with th siege of Thebes and the fatal duel between the two sons. Man other playwrights in that era used the Oedipus story.

Sophocles wrote *Oedipus the King* at the height of his ca reer as a dramatist. Although Aristotle, a century later, chos it as the masterpiece of Greek tragedy, this most durable o Greek plays did not, at its initial showing, receive first prize We know that Sophocles wrote what might be called the las act of the Oedipus drama, *Oedipus at Colonus,* years later. shall argue that *Oedipus the King* needs this last act and that in terms of both theater and the underlying myth, the tw plays should be performed together to be fully understood.

After the great period of Greek drama the Oedipus stor continued to march vigorously through the centuries. Talente actors in all ages have been especially attracted to the role o Oedipus. Polus, for example, the most famous actor of th fourth century, was especially renowned for his performance in both *Oedipus the King* and *Oedipus at Colonus.* During th fourth century B.C. the level of dramatic writing had declined while the art of acting and the importance of individual actor rose. In fact, as actors became more influential they tended t modify the classical dramas in order to give themselves mor attractive roles. Finally Lycurgus, who was famous for re building the theater of Dionysus and for his patronage of th ancient drama, put a stop to this tampering with Athens' clas sical heritage by ordering that state copies of all the tragedie be deposited in the archives and that a fine be imposed on anyone who changed the scripts.

In succeeding centuries, classical tragedy, comedy, and satyr plays were performed in Greece—in fact, throughout the whole Hellenized world. Early in the third century B.C. the actors were organized into guilds, with a priest of Dionysus at their head. Since these guilds were religious organizations, members were exempt from military service and taxes, and were permitted to travel in foreign countries. As a result, Greek drama was performed as far west as Italy and Sicily, as well as in the eastern Mediterranean and Egypt. Unfortunately, we have little evidence as to the choice of plays, although Euripides seems to be mentioned most often.*

Greece fell under Roman rule in 146 B.C., but the Greek theater maintained a quasi-independence and enjoyed immense popularity throughout the empire well into the second century A.D. From what records we have of Roman productions, the story of Oedipus—in Sophocles' version as well as others—continued an active life in the theater of the Graeco-Roman world for another four hundred years. Classical scholars are fond of noting that Julius Caesar as a young man tried his hand as a playwright and wrote his own *Oedipus Rex*. The Emperor Nero acted Oedipus in a production of the Sophoclean play, and Seneca wrote a very dull but influential *Oedipus Rex*. Though Seneca introduced as much gore as might be expected from a gladiatorial combat, he managed to produce at the same time the least dramatic of all the extant versions.

In the so-called Dark Ages, Greek tragedies faded from the consciousness of the West, although they continued to be performed for several centuries in the Byzantine Empire. A fragment of a bas-relief in the Hermitage, circa 500 A.D., shows scenes from *Medea* and *Oedipus,* and there are records of other performances to the end of the seventh century.

Early in the fifteenth century, Greek tragedies in manuscript

* In the middle of the third century B.C., records show that three classical tragedies (together with new plays) were given at the dramatic contests in Athens, instead of only one fifth-century classic—the rule a hundred years earlier. This suggests to some scholars that classical tragedy became *more* rather than *less* important at this time. It is reasonable to assume that Sophocles' *Oedipus* continued to be popular.

began to reach Italy–brought by adventurous scholars from Byzantium. The most famous of these scholars, Giovanni Aurispa, literally sold the clothes off his back in Constantinople in order to bring back to Venice a booty of two hundred and thirty-eight manuscripts, including six tragedies of Aeschylus and seven of Sophocles. These tragedians as well as Euripides were edited and printed by Aldus, the Venetian scholar and Hellenist. Sophocles was the first to be published, in 1502.

The modern theatrical life of *Oedipus the King* may be said to have begun rather precisely in Vicenza on March 3, 1585, when the Sophoclean tragedy was performed amid much pomp at the opening of the famous Teatro Olimpico of Palladio. The play was presented in an admirable Italian translation by the Venetian scholar and statesman Orsatto Giustiniani, with music by Andrea Gabrieli, organist at the Cathedral of San Marco. "It was fitting," wrote Filippo Pigafetta, a member of the first audience, "that this most renowned theater in the world should have as its first presentation the most excellent tragedy in the world."

In a delightful and learned study, Professor Leo Schrade, of the University of Bâle, has traced the history of this production in detail. Actors were of the top rank, the costumes were sumptuous, and celebrated Italian artists designed the set. Angelo Ingegneri, the director, rejected the idea of *cothurni* and masks and insisted on "modern" (i.e., sixteenth-century) acting. He was especially interested in the role of the chorus in tragedy and insisted that music for the odes be kept simple so that every word could be understood. Either because he did not know that the Greek chorus both danced and sang or because he rejected the idea for the sixteenth-century Italian stage, the chorus remained motionless, chanting their lines without instrumental accompaniment. Gabrieli's music for the chorus is extant.

It is interesting to note that questions of translation and production that were discussed then are still being discussed today. Should the chorus sing or speak? Is the chorus "an agreeable ornament" or an essential part of the play? If the latter, how should its lines and participation in the action be handled? Should sets and costumes imitate the ancient mode or should they be "modern"?

In 1962, nearly four hundred years after the historic opening of the Teatro Olimpico, this theater was once again the setting for a memorable production of *Oedipus*. The director was Alexis Minotis, of the Greek National Theater, the Italian translation was supplied by Quasimodo, and the music was composed by Minotis' wife, the Greek actress Katina Paxinou. A reviewer called it "a very grand occasion," adding "[it was] something more, for it showed that Greek tragedy need not survive on our stages as a mere cultural relic . . . *a whole new dimension of dramatic experience lies open.*" (Emphasis supplied.)

With the 1585 Vicenza performance, *Oedipus* was launched in the modern theater. Later, in the classical period of the French theater, Corneille wrote his own version, adding a love plot. Racine considered competing with Sophocles, but refrained. Voltaire wrote an *Oedipe,* turning the play into an anticlerical tract, with the prophet Tiresias a venal and corrupt priest.

Both the Sophoclean tragedy and the myth have continued to fascinate French writers up to the present time. Gide wrote a modern version, *Oedipe,* and Cocteau dealt with the Oedipus theme on no less than four occasions. Cocteau translated the Greek play in 1925, and later, at the request of Stravinsky, wrote a version in six episodes, with narrator, to be set to music. (The Cocteau script was translated into Church Latin, and Cocteau served as narrator on several occasions.) In 1934, Cocteau used the myth again in *The Infernal Machine*. Finally, he composed a version for dance and mime which was first produced in 1962.

In England, Dryden and Lee wrote a translation of Sophocles' *Oedipus,* effectively bowdlerizing all the shocking elements of the plot. Only in the nineteenth century, however, did *Oedipus* really begin his return to the modern theater—in preparation, it might be said, for something far more explosive and significant in the twentieth century. Performances in ancient Greek began to multiply in the universities in the middle of the nineteenth century and have continued up to the present day. There were many notable performances in the United States, in England, and on the Continent. Sir Richard Jebb, greatest of English Sophoclean scholars, crossed the Atlantic in 1888 to see the play given at Harvard. He includes an account of it in his famous—and still the best—edition of the play. Whether in the original or in the vernacular, these performances in the theater introduced a new idea of Greek plays, an idea which seemed revolutionary and positively subversive to some classical scholars: that *Oedipus* and other Greek plays could only be fully understood in the theater, not in the library! The idea is still scorned by a dwindling number of regressive classicists. As part of this modernization movement, translations appeared in more or less speakable versions, often to the horror of the purely philological.

Perhaps the two most famous productions of *Oedipus* in the late nineteenth and early twentieth centuries were those of the great French actor Mounet-Sully and of the German producer Max Reinhardt. Members of the audience who saw his performance say that Mounet-Sully's Oedipus was the greatest theatrical experience of their lives. In a generation when great actors played all the leading roles in the classics, from Shakespeare to Ibsen, Mounet-Sully believed his Oedipus to be (and he is supported by the testimony of contemporary critics) his greatest role. Mounet-Sully's first performance of *Oedipus* took place in a Roman amphitheater in the south of France; he was to play that role for many years, well into the twentieth century. He even made a silent movie of the play, without cutting the original.

Reinhardt's *Oedipus* exploded on the scene in 1910 in the Circus Schumann in Berlin, and again in 1919 in the gigantic Grosse Schulspielhaus. Though it used a German translation of Sophocles' text, the production was sheer Reinhardt, a mighty spectacle, complete with milling crowds and fervent realism in scenic and sound effects. Later, Reinhardt brought his production to England.

One theatergoer who was present at both the Mounet-Sully and the Reinhardt productions was J. T. Sheppard, the distinguished Greek scholar, then a young man and fellow of King's College, Cambridge. His comments were obviously written out of emotion, and with ideas that came to him in the theater and not in his Cambridge study.

Of Reinhardt's production he wrote: "That performance taught me that the strength of the plot makes the play great and exciting even in the worst conditions that a bad producer can invent."

Of Mounet-Sully's performance, which he saw in Paris, he said: "Because of its formal beauty, the French production is an inspiration to all who care for drama, and a proof that Greek drama, not bolstered up by sensationalism and with sentimentality, has power to hold and to move a modern audience. If you doubt whether in these days Greek tragedy still matters, you may learn the answer in Paris."

One great stumbling block to the revival of *Oedipus* in the modern world has been the matter of translation. In England there was particularly strong opposition to translating Greek drama into the vernacular. The universities were saying: If you want to read *Oedipus,* learn Greek. And the Victorian Establishment considered the story of a man who kills his father and marries his mother far too shocking for English ears and eyes. But toward the end of the nineteenth century, Oxford undergraduates asked the university authorities for permission to start a theater in which Greek plays could be performed in translation. Jowett, then Master of Balliol, supported this radical proposal. It squeaked by the authorities, but only with the proviso that a play should be performed in the original Greek once every three years. But the taboo against the "indecent" elements in Greek myth died hard. As late as 1912, the English actor Sir Martin Harvey found that Dryden's version of *Oedipus* was thought to be the best. Dissatisfied, he was about to commission a new translation of Sophocles, with additional explanatory scenes on Oedipus' early life, when the Lord Chancellor refused to license such a play.

The "translation dam," however, was cracking. Gilbert Murray, with his enormous prestige as a scholar and his uncanny facility for turning ancient Greek into acceptable Victorian rhythms, made the first great breech. It was Murray's translation of *Oedipus* that Reinhardt used when he gave the production which Sheppard saw. In 1923, Sir Martin Harvey used Murray's translation when he played the part in London and New York.

But for the emergence of *Oedipus the King* as living drama in the English-speaking theater the name of an Irish poet is more important than Murray's. For it was William Butler

Yeats's version of the play, first performed in the Abbey Theatre, that was to become the orthodox script for producers. In 1933, the Abbey gave one performance of *Oedipus* during their season in New York, with Yeats himself making the introductory speech. In 1945, Lawrence Olivier used the Yeats version for his production at the Old Vic; it was seen in New York the following year. The Yeats version was also chosen by Tyrone Guthrie for the Stratford, Ontario, summer seasons in 1954 and 1955, and every year I come across new productions using this script.

Two points are worth making about Yeats's translation–or, more properly, his translation and adaptation of Sophocles' play. First, it is written in simple, melodious English prose. Knowing little or no Greek, Yeats appears to have used the best available "trot," Jebb's literal translation, and turned the dialogue into short, rhythmic speeches. The longer speeches of the original version are cut drastically–including ninety lines from the last and crucial scene of the play. I am indebted to Bernard Knox for calling my attention to these points about Yeats's version. As for the choruses, Yeats wrote singable Irish poems for the few strophes he did not omit entirely. And yet, because he was both a poet and a playwright, Yeats did more than anyone else to launch *Oedipus the King* into the English-speaking theater.

The real *Oedipus* explosion, however, both in translation and performance, came only after the Second World War. Popular reading of Greek tragedy in translation has increased prodigiously in all Western countries, especially in the last five years. In number of translations and in number of readers the English language leads all the rest, although excellent new versions are appearing in French, Italian, and modern Greek.

Two particularly significant productions of *Oedipus* were noticed for the period before the Second World War. What about the much larger number which have been staged since the war? I select two. My first is the Tyrone Guthrie production in Canada, later widely seen in the United States on television and as a movie. My second is the production (known now throughout most of the modern world) by the Greek National Theater with Alexis Minotis as director and in the leading role.

The Stratford production ran for two summers in repertory with several plays of Shakespeare. My calculation is that it was probably seen and heard by more persons than ever witnessed any other Greek play in English up to that time. Yet, superficially, one might guess that Guthrie's staging would have kept modern theatergoers away in droves. Actors wore larger-than-life masks, so no changes of expression were possible. And they moved slowly across the stage in thick-soled boots designed to resemble ancient *cothurni.*

Guthrie has written brilliantly of the reasoning behind his staging of *Oedipus* and gives, I think, the key to its acceptance by large audiences. He was not aiming at historical accuracy or an imitation of the productions of 2500 years ago. His sole purpose was to use any means–which explains his experiment with masks–to escape the literal in time and place. He was seeking–and I think he found in large measure–what he called the universal quality of tragedy lifted to an "abstracted and remote grandeur."

It is unlikely that many directors will imitate Guthrie's Stratford experiment. But it brought an authentic theatrical experience of the *Oedipus* tragedy to many, and only a handful who saw the play considered it an exercise in virtuosity. Excellent acting under admirable direction achieved the larger-than-life tone to a remarkable degree. The chorus, though lacking the plasticity and integration Minotis achieves in Greece, was better than most. Yeats's version was spoken effectively, but his drastic cutting of dialogue and choral odes–though it made the director's task an easier one–subtracted from the full tragic dimensions of the play.

My own experience in witnessing this production was, I think, typical. For the first few minutes I noticed the masks and other curious imports from antiquity. Then quite suddenly I forgot them. Several scenes from the Guthrie production I remember with emotion: Oedipus' towering passion when he accuses Creon of plotting against his life; the depths of agony and fear in his scenes with Jocasta and later with the herdsman, when the appalling truth of his guilt begins to terrify his soul; and, finally, the scene of ultimate purgation when, self-blinded, Oedipus bursts through the palace doors for the final confrontation with Creon, the chorus, and his own children.

In all of these strategic turning points of the play, every depth, every nuance of emotion is conveyed solely by words, by bodily movement, or by gesture. Here, acting seems to enter a different realm, where facial expression is no longer needed. One of the most striking and successful novelties in Guthrie's staging is the device by which he conveys Oedipus' blindness. Instead of the usual streaks of blood-red paint upon eyes and face, which somehow project a false realism rather than tragic horror, Oedipus enters with his head and shoulders shrouded in a thick black veil, letting the imagination of the audience supply the sense of total blindness and disaster.

The second example of a towering modern production is that of Minotis and the Greek National Theater. Alexis Minotis has directed and acted in *Oedipus the King* in Greece, in the United States, in France, in Italy, and at the Edinburgh Theater Festival. But it is only at the ancient Greek theater at Epidaurus that one can fully experience Minotis' *Oedipus*.

To begin with, the setting is dramatic and beautiful: fifty-five tiers of seats rise against Mt. Kynortion and look out over an expanse of tall cypresses and olive groves, where lie the ruins of a temple to Aesculapius and a vast complex of other buildings devoted to his cult and the cure of the sick. Epidaurus is famous for having the best-preserved round orchestra of any of the theaters of antiquity. In the center is the stone "thymele," or altar, which even today no Greek actor dare desecrate by stepping on. A two-story stage has been reconstructed on the far side, where most of the dialogue is spoken. The audience gathers slowly; there are tourists from abroad, but they lose themselves in the crowd. Front-row seats are reserved, as in Sophocles' time, for Greek and foreign dignitaries, but Greeks of all classes arrive in big American-built cars and in ramshackle local buses. Peasant women in black skirts with white kerchiefs round their heads come with their mustached men. They climb the fifty-five tiers to the cheaper seats, but the miraculous acoustics of the theater bring every word of the play even to those in the last rows.

The formal quality of "universal and high tragedy" which Guthrie sought so earnestly seems to have been infused without effort into the productions at Epidaurus. The Greek directors scorn such external antiquities as masks and *cothurni.*

ing out of the naturalistic theater. Of many examples these may be cited: the rediscovery and continuing interest in the corpus of Brecht's plays with their so-called "epic" style; the plays of Becket, Ionesco, Genet and some of the early Albee, as well as the Royal Shakespeare Theater's recent attempt to find a less realistic style for their production of *King Lear*.

The chorus is, of course, the most formal element in Greek tragedy. Until recently it has been the despair of modern producers of Greek plays. Most directors have solved the problem in one of three ways: They have cut the chorus, leaving only a few spoken lines which the plot absolutely required; they have turned it into a disorganized crowd (the Reinhardt production is an extreme example); or they have taught the cast to recite the odes in monotonous unison while making a few movements that were totally unrelated to the style of the rest of the play. Many years ago Thornton Wilder told me why he hated modern performances of Greek drama. "The chorus always reminds me of a bunch of Vassar girls in nightgowns," he lamented. This was the period when the audience sighed with relief when the choral episodes were over. The general feeling was: "Thank God, we can now get on with the play."

Since then two things have happened. The Greek National Theater in Athens has learned—by dedication and experiment—to make the tragic chorus a living and integral part of each play they produce. And, either in imitation or in response to their own sense of theater, directors in other countries are learning how to bring the Greek chorus to life.

Apart from present-day interest in the staging of ancient drama, the Greek chorus poses a deeper question. Playwrights in all ages have felt the need to provide their own functional substitutes for its role. The word "chorus" is misleading to modern ears. It is true that the Greek choruses, like those in modern musical plays, both sing and dance, but their true function is much more complex. It has been defined as that of "commentator." This is too limited and didactic, but it helps. Wilder himself, from the time he wrote the Stage Manager into *Our Town*, has been searching for and using substitutes for a chorus. Shakespeare had half a dozen devices to do what the chorus of fifteen men or women did for every fifth-century Greek play. He used comic characters and fools, but, above all, he used his major characters, whose practice it was to step out of the flow of the plot to soliloquize on what "the times" or the hearts of men everywhere (if they could be articulate) would think of the action or tell of its meaning in some eternal dimension. These are all functions of a proper chorus in the Sophoclean sense. Bernard Shaw so desperately needed a chorus that he solved the problem–or, rather, failed to solve it–by writing prefaces.

My dogmatic summing up is that, when plays grow serious and touch on deeper issues, the chorus reappears in one guise or another. I would argue further that the choral scenes in *Oedipus* and other Greek plays–when staged as some modern directors are learning to stage them–far from being a hazard for the box office, are becoming an asset.

The best statement I have heard concerning the relationship of chorus to actor to play was made to me by Alexis Minotis just after I saw him in *Oedipus* at Epidaurus:

"The chorus in all Greek plays has definite form–it isn't the people, but it *represents* the people, in mythical, stylized form. That is our theory. And that is where Reinhardt was wrong when he produced *Oedipus* in Germany and made it a spectacle. And that is where even Mounet-Sully was wrong. They both confused crowds of people with the chorus.

"We look upon Greek tragedy as moving on two planes, the vertical and the horizontal. The vertical is the plane of the hero, or protagonist, and the other leading characters. The horizontal is the plane of the chorus. Its movement on that plane is forward and backward, like the surf of the sea. Both planes intersect, and both are necessary to create the play. The dramatic action occurs. The chorus is present but silent; then, from that action, they take the materials to create poetry before your eyes. The chorus does not come in from the wings and move on and off the stage. It is present almost all the time, absorbing the dramatic action and then turning it into poetry and into dance. . . . The chorus in each play differs from that in every other play. They are composed in different styles –and, indeed, it requires a whole kaleidoscope of different styles to make a Greek play. If you were to remove the chorus, what would be left? There would be, I would say, merely a modern play."

But I would now quarrel with Minotis about his last statement. Today modern playwrights, as I have suggested, with great ingenuity and imagination are seeking–and finding–equivalents for the ancient chorus.

NOTE ON TRANSLATION

This writer's version of *Oedipus the King* and *Oedipus at Colonus* aims at a script that can be spoken by actors and read as a play. How faithful is it to the Greek? Or how free is it in translating Greek poetry into English? Only audiences or readers who know both English and Greek can answer such questions. It is my hope, first, that these plays emerge as close to their originals as the differences in language, culture, and conventions permit. And, second, that this is a script as free as is necessary to make them speak as plays–sometimes in prose, sometimes in poetry–to modern readers and audiences.

Oedipus the King

OEDIPUS THE KING

Cast of Characters

OEDIPUS, King of Thebes
JOCASTA, Queen and wife of OEDIPUS
CREON, brother of JOCASTA
TIRESIAS, a blind prophet
CORINTHIAN MESSENGER
A HERDSMAN
MESSENGER (from inside the palace)
ANTIGONE and ISMENE, young children, daughters of OEDIPUS and JOCASTA
PRIEST OF ZEUS
CROWD OF THEBANS: men, women, and children
ATTENDANTS, GUARDS, etc.
CHORUS of Theban elders, representing the people of Thebes
CHORUS LEADER*

Scene: before the palace of Oedipus, King of Thebes. In front an altar surrounded by a crowd of suppliants–men, women, and children, led by the Priest of Zeus. They are all carrying olive branches, which they place upon the altar.

(*The great central doors of the palace open and* OEDIPUS *enters.*)

OEDIPUS

O my children–
newest generation from old Cadmus born,

* The Leader sometimes speaks for the whole chorus, sometimes as an individual. Modern directors frequently assign some of the lines of the chorus–or of the Leader–to other members of the chorus.

Cadmus who founded our city–
why do you sit here with suppliant boughs?
What prayers have you for me now?
The sky smokes with incense from our altars;
the air is shaken with the people's cries for help and
healing,
and with our lamentations for the dead.

I, Oedipus, known to all men–and they call me great–
have come here to learn all–
not from another, but with my own eyes and ears.

Now, Old Man, speak to me–
for it is right that you speak for all.
Tell me the kind of supplication that you make.
From fear do you come?
Or to seek some benefit?
All my desire is to help to the utmost.
Flint-hearted would I be, did I not listen
in pity to your prayers.

PRIEST

Oedipus, mighty master of my fatherland,
we have come as supplicants to your altars,
and, as you see, both old and young.
Some of us mere children without strong wings to fly far;
some have come weighed down with years.
I am the priest of Zeus;
these, here, have been chosen
from the youth of the city.
Others, crowned with garlands,
sit in the market place
at the two temples of Athena;
and other suppliants have gathered
by the prophetic fires of Apollo.

All this because the city,
as you see, plunges into the depths

like a ship staggering at sea.
Storm-driven, she cannot raise her head
above the bloody surge.
For the land is blasted!
Blasted in the bud the country's crops;
blasted the cattle in our fields;
blasted the seed in the barren wombs of women.
The god of fire and fever has brought this deadly plague,
swooped and struck the city.
And so dark Hades abounds in groans and lamentation.
Neither I, nor these children here,
consider that you are a god, Oedipus,
but we do count you first among men—
skilled in human affairs,
but also in dealings with the gods.
For you came to this city of Thebes
and delivered us from the bloody tribute
paid to that savage songstress.
You rid us of the Sphinx.
And this you did with no guidance from us,
but, as all believe, through some god's help
you restored the city and gave us life again.

So now, O Oedipus, mightiest in the eyes of all,
we and these suppliants beseech you:
Find for us succor and salvation,
whether through God's word or man's knowledge.
I know this: Plans based on experience
such as yours with men and gods
will prosper. So, noblest of men, lift us up.
Make the city stand upright once more!
Take care for yourself too.
Today the country still lauds you as savior,
remembers your services of old, which were mighty indeed.
Oh, may future generations
never look back upon your rule to say:
Oedipus lifted up the state, then let it fall.
No! Restore and stablish the city

in certain safety once more!
You brought us fortune and heaven's honor.
Be equal to this ordeal again.
How much better to rule a land
and govern a city full of men,
than a kingdom empty of life.
A ship without sailors is not a ship;
a city without citizens, no city.

OEDIPUS

My pitiable children,
I know fully why you have come
and the desire of your hearts.
You are ill, all of you, I know well,
but none have a sickness like mine.
For you are ill each man to himself.
But my sick soul groans for myself,
for the city, and for you.
You did not wake me out of sleep, my children,
be sure of that–I have wept much, and
sent my mind searching a hundred byways of care and grief.
And I have found the only cure
and acted upon my finding.

Creon, my brother-in-law,
I sent to Apollo's temple to inquire:
What word, what deed by me
would save the city?
(*With impatience*)
Now, as I reckon his time away–
What is he doing? He should be here!
Well,
when he comes,
I would be traitor and coward
did I not act in all points as the god commands.

PRIEST

O my lord, what good words you have spoken. These men here have just signaled: Creon is coming!

OEDIPUS

O Lord Apollo! I see light shining in his face and eyes. Perhaps he comes too with the light of luck and salvation for us.

PRIEST

You must be right, my lord, for he comes with a rich crown of laurel on his head!

OEDIPUS

Well, soon we shall see—he is within earshot now.
(CREON *enters.*)
Creon, my own kinsman, O son of Monoecius, what message from the god?

CREON

A good word, Oedipus. If these harsh events turn out favorably, all our affairs will prosper.

OEDIPUS

Creon, what sort of oracle is that! From this message of yours I can neither take heart nor warning.

CREON

Do you wish all these people standing by to hear the god's words? If so, I will speak. If not, we can go inside the palace.

OEDIPUS

Proclaim the word to all! I am more grieved and anxious for their lives than for my own.

CREON

Then I shall speak what I heard from the god. Lord Apollo clearly and openly commands us to drive pollution from the land. It has been nourished here. Let it grow no longer, for it is our death.

OEDIPUS

What sort of cleansing or expiation is called for? What is the nature of this pollution?

CREON

Murder. The guilty must be banished, or the crime expiated, by the blood of the murderers. It is the blood of the murdered man, Oedipus, which has brought this storm of misfortune upon the state!

OEDIPUS

Who, what sort and condition of man was murdered, according to the god?

CREON

A king. King Laius, my lord, who governed this country before you came.

OEDIPUS

I knew him well, of course, through the reports of others.

CREON

The god now clearly bids us wreak vengeance on his murderers.

OEDIPUS

But where on earth may the murderers be found? The clues themselves will be hard to find, harder still to unravel for a crime so old.

CREON

The clues are here in Thebes! What we look for can be found if we give our whole mind to this inquiry.

OEDIPUS

Tell me, was King Laius at home, or in the country, or in some foreign land when he was murdered?

CREON

He was on a holy mission—to consult the oracle. Reported returning, but not yet home, when he was killed.

OEDIPUS

Surely some herald or companion saw the crime. From him we could learn something which might help.

CREON

Yes, companions–but all except one ran in terror. Of what he saw he had but one useful thing to report.

OEDIPUS

What? One clue might lead to many. Let us make a small beginning, then we may hope.

CREON

Robbers, he said, several, fell upon the escort. Many hands, not the blow of one man, killed the king.

OEDIPUS

(*Thinking*)

No robber would have nerved himself for such a killing, had he not been bribed.

CREON

That was considered also. But when King Laius met his death no one took up the case, for we were all in deep trouble.

OEDIPUS

What sort of trouble could have prevented a full inquiry into the death of a king–and a king dying as King Laius died?

CREON

The riddling Sphinx–who brought the plague upon us–made us dismiss the mystery of the king's death, and think only of the evils at our feet.

OEDIPUS

Well, then, starting afresh I will discover and make manifest this mystery. It is fitting that Apollo, and that you too, turn now your mind to this man's death. And you will find me a righteous ally in wreaking vengeance, an ally both of Thebes and of the god. So I make this proclamation not only because my friends have an interest, but for my own sake. Any man who kills one king might kill another and try his hand on me. So if I do my full duty to the murdered man, I also serve myself. And now, my children, make all haste, rise and lift up your suppliant boughs. Let someone of you go, and assemble here the people of the city. For I have done all things needful. And it will be known soon whether we have failed in this enterprise, or with the god's help have won success and salvation.

(CREON *goes out to the side,* OEDIPUS *into the palace.*)

PRIEST

O children, stand! For the king has published to us all the things we came to hear. And Apollo, you who have sent us the divine oracle, be our savior now and cause the sickness in the land to cease.

(PRIEST *and crowd of suppliants leave. Enter from the side the* CHORUS *of fifteen elders, representing the people of the city. They sing first of the Delphic oracle, then call upon the gods for help and protection against the plague.*)

CHORUS

O melodious word of God,
what message do you bring
to shining Thebes? What word
from Pytho rich in gold? Racked am I,
my soul in terror trembling–
O savior, healer of Delos, hail!
Tell me, in my dread,
what end you will fulfill?
Must we pay new debts,
or are old penances
renewed out of the revolving years?
Oh, tell me, word of heaven;
oh, tell me, child of golden hope!

And first on you I call,
daughter of Zeus, immortal Athena,
and on your sister Artemis,
this land's protector.
Behold, in the midst of our market
you sit high on your throne,

goddess of fair fame.
And Phoebus Apollo, on you I cry,
far shooter of the arrows.
Be manifest in your triple power
to fight off the doom of death
for me. Do this, if ever in past years you
drove the burning pest away,
when ruin sprang on our city–
oh, come to us now, and save.

Without number the pains I bear
for all the people sicken,
and their sickness is my sickness.
Thinking is no gain for me, and in
my soul no sword of salvation.
Behold, in our noble country
no crops and no children replenish the earth;
women labor,
but no life is born of the pain.
Rather all creatures
like birds on the wing,
endlessly move to the shore,
swifter than fire,
swifter than implacable fire,
to the shore of the western god.

O my city,
with the multitude of these dead
you die,
and pitilessly are stretched upon the earth
the bodies of your sons–
death-bearing–and no one laments them.
Rather, wives and old mothers with whitened hair
from every quarter of the town come forth
to cling to the steps of altars.
Bitterly, moan on moan they pile,
and beg surcease from pain.
So litany for healing
rings out through the city
to merge with tongues of grief.

From all of these evils
give us rescue and relief,
O golden daughter of Zeus!
In the midst of death,
grant us the fair countenance of courage.

Ares, raging destroyer, god of death,
you slay my body, not with the spear of bronze,
but with fury of a burning sickness.
Men as in battle cry out and fall–
O Zeus, turn this death god backward
in driven flight from my country.
Let him be blown far, far,
out to the vast sea room
of Amphitrite,
or to the barbarous Thracian wave.
For what soul escapes death
in the night season,
day will destroy him.
O Lord, O wielder of the lightning's power,
who charge your bolts with flame's fury,
O Zeus, father, smite,
smite the death god with thy thunder's doom.

And Lykian Apollo, Lord of Light,
oh, from your bowstring's twisted gold
rain down all-slaughtering
your arrows
upon Death, our enemy.
Let them be before us as our defense.
And, too, the torches of Artemis with
which she scours the Lycean hills,
may they lighten and protect us!
Now you I call upon,
Bacchus, with your head banded in gold,
your cheek wine-red,
name-giver to my fatherland–
you and your maenads–
Evoi! Evoi! Let all the torches in your hand
blaze brightly and bring us salvation.

Bacchus, be our ally against Ares, the
divinity without honor;
fight with us
the shameful god of death!

(*During the last lines* OEDIPUS *enters from the palace.*)

OEDIPUS

You have begged for help.
Listen and welcome my words.
Do what this sickness demands,
you will have strength and succor,
and the plague be lifted.
I shall with your help make search and inquiry, for
the story of this case is strange to me.
Certainly without some clue from others
I could hardly track down a crime so ancient.
But since that time I am no longer stranger here,
but a citizen among citizens. And so
I make this proclamation to all men of Thebes:
Who amongst you has any knowledge
of who killed Laius, the son of Labdacus,
I command him to reveal all.
And if he fear to speak, being himself guilty,
yet I bid him testify. For so
he will escape the extreme penalty,
suffer no harm more terrible than banishment.
Further, if any of you know some alien
from a foreign shore as the murderer,
let him speak. He shall have a reward in substance
and my grace besides.

But if any keep his lips sealed,
if any reject my command
to shield a friend, or fearing for himself,
hear now my judgment:
I decree that no one in this dominion which I rule
receive this person into his home,
speak to him ever, share with him prayer or sacrifice,
or family libation.

Rather, I command all men
to thrust him from their homes–
for he who repudiates me
shields the very pollution that we suffer,
as the Pythian god has now revealed.
By this act and proclamation
I become ally of the god himself
and of the murdered man!

On the murderer, on the creature
who did the deed, I lay this curse
and imprecation, whether the doer be one man
who did the deed alone or with accomplices.
I pray he wear out his rotten life
in evil days and die accursed of God.
And I add this imprecation:
That I myself,
if ever I had this man in my home
and knew him there,
I too suffer the same abominable curse
I have laid upon him.

All this I bid you execute,
for my sake, for the sake of the god,
and for the sake of the country,
blasted as it is to barrenness and hated of the gods.
For even if the divine were not in this,
it were shameful to leave the crime a mystery.
The murdered man was noble–
and, besides, your king. So
you must search it out to the end.

I, too, will search it out,
for I hold the reins of royal power
which he once held and am married to his queen.
How close to the murdered man I stand!
Closer still I might have been
had she borne children to us both;
but in offspring he was unblest, for
fate swooped down and cut him off.

So I shall act in this ordeal
as though he were my father,
taking every means to seek, to seize, the murderer,
murderer of Labdacus' son, who was the son of Polydorus,
son of Cadmus,
who was Agenor's son of ancient time.

And for those disobedient to my commands
I beseech the god
visit them with punishments:
May heaven give no produce to their fields,
no babes to the wombs of their women,
and may they perish by the curse I have invoked—
or, if there be a fate more terrible,
may it be theirs!

But to you, citizens of Thebes,
and all who accept my words,
let justice be your ally, and may the gods
be gracious to you now and forever.

CHORUS LEADER

Since you have put me under oath to give you the truth, I will speak. I did not kill the king, nor can I point to his murderer. As to this inquiry—should not Apollo, who declared the oracle, tell us who did the deed?

OEDIPUS

A just opinion. But to compel gods against their wills—no man has power.

CHORUS LEADER

Then could I suggest a second course?

OEDIPUS

Yes, and if you have a third, speak out.

CHORUS LEADER

I know a man whose seeing eye is like Apollo's. He is the Lord Tiresias. Anyone who asks through him will learn with certainty the truth.

OEDIPUS

This has not been forgotten. For since Creon declared to us the oracle, I have sent, I have twice sent for the prophet. And, I am amazed, still he is not here!

CHORUS LEADER

His skill will help—but there are certain earlier rumors about the murder, almost faded now from the minds of men.

OEDIPUS

What rumors? I shall neglect nothing.

CHORUS LEADER

Well, it was said he was killed by several robbers—

OEDIPUS

So I have heard. But the survivor who witnessed the crime—no one has seen him!

CHORUS LEADER

No, but I believe the murderer, if he has a shred of fear when he hears your curse, will reveal himself.

OEDIPUS

No—the man who did not shrink from that crime will not shudder at my curse.

CHORUS LEADER

Now the seer who will convict the murderer is here. They are bringing the holy prophet! Above all other mortals he can divine the truth!

(*Enter* TIRESIAS *led by a boy.*)

OEDIPUS

O Tiresias, seer and searcher of all knowledge and all mystery, in heaven and on the earth: Look upon our city. You cannot with your eyes, but with your mind you see and know the plague affecting us. We have found you out, my lord, our first citizen and our only hope. You may not have heard the report of the messenger, but to our mission Apollo has sent his answer: From the plague there is only one hope of deliverance–to search and find the murderers of Laius. And then we kill them, or from the country drive them into exile. So, we beseech you, do not grudge us words of augury, or prophet's art, or any other pathway to the truth you know. Save yourself, save the state and me–oh, save us all from this dead man's pollution. For man to help man out of trouble with every outward power, and his soul's strength–that is nobility.

TIRESIAS

Oh, how terrible for a wise man to have wisdom–when wisdom brings no good–

(*Muttering to himself*)

I knew this thing so perfectly–but then it faded from my mind. Had I remembered, I had never, never come.

OEDIPUS

But you have come. Why with so faint a heart?

TIRESIAS

Send me home. If you do–and trust me–you can bear your burden easily–

(*To himself*)

And I can bear mine.

OEDIPUS

A strange, unnatural speech! By denying us the oracle, you are unfriendly to your fatherland.

TIRESIAS

Ah, this is no time for you to speak such words–and if I spoke, your suffering would be mine.

OEDIPUS

(*Shouting*)

In heaven's name, do not deny us the knowledge which you have! We are all suppliants. On our knees we beg you!

(OEDIPUS *and the* OTHER CITIZENS, *all on their knees to* TIRESIAS)

TIRESIAS

(*In a quiet voice, almost sadly*)
Not one. Now I see. Not one of you understands. And of this be sure: Never will I show forth these evils that I know in my heart. For if I did they would be your disasters and mine too.

OEDIPUS

(*Thoroughly aroused*)
What, in God's name, are you saying? Knowing what will save us you refuse to speak? Tiresias, what you have conceived in your heart is treason to me, and for the city ruin and death!

TIRESIAS

Let me say this to you. I shall not further torture myself–or you. I advise you–this is a futile examination.
(*Pronouncing his words very slowly*)
From me you'll never learn anything–

OEDIPUS

(*Beside himself*)
No! No! O creature of hell! O fiend implacable! You would make angry a heart of stone–

(TIRESIAS *continues to speak to himself words which cannot be understood.*)

Are you still muttering, unmoved, unmoved?

TIRESIAS

(*Lifting his blind eyes to* OEDIPUS)
You reproach me for my anger. But you cannot see the living fury in your own soul–

OEDIPUS

Who would not be angry, hearing these words with which you shame the city?

TIRESIAS

My words speak of events, Oedipus, which will come to pass–
(*He pauses.*)

will come to pass, even though I, secretly and in silence, were to bury all of them.

OEDIPUS

Then, if they will come to pass, speak them out–yes, speak them out you must!

TIRESIAS

(*Quietly*)

No. I will say no more than I have said.

(*Raising his voice a little*)

So, to your heart's content, rage on; burst into fury, if you will–

OEDIPUS

I will! Yes, I will unlock the fullness of my rage. And tell your utmost infamy, which I know well. You yourself contrived the murder. I believe that, yes, and did the deed, except perhaps your own hand did not kill him, because you are blind. Indeed, were it not for that infirmity I'd say that you alone, no other, murdered him.

TIRESIAS

(*Trembling*)

So . . . so . . . so . . . Then I bid you: Honor the proclamation which you made. And speak no word from this day forth. None to the Thebans here, none to me, since it is yourself that is the unclean creature–it is *you* who pollute the land.

OEDIPUS

Oh, shameful insolence! To bark blackmail at your king! How can you think to escape–

TIRESIAS

I *have* escaped. I am invulnerable, Oedipus. For I nourish in my soul the strength of truth.

OEDIPUS

Truth! Your prophet's craft never taught it to you. By whom were you taught?

TIRESIAS

By you! I was unwilling to speak the truth till you compelled me.

OEDIPUS

Speak what? Repeat, that I may know quite certainly what you have been saying.

TIRESIAS

You understood. This is a taunt to provoke me into telling more.

OEDIPUS

(*Slowly*)

No, not perfectly did I understand before. Pronounce the words again.

TIRESIAS

(*Also speaking slowly*)

You, you are the killer of the murdered king. You are the man whom in this search of yours you seek to find.

OEDIPUS

Tiresias, now you will no longer mock me–

(*Advancing as if to seize him*)

but pay in pain for all this calumny. And for twice speaking it.

TIRESIAS

Oh? Then I'll pile more on top of the other–that you may be the more angry.

OEDIPUS

As much as you like, prophet, since all your words are emptiness.

TIRESIAS

(*Loudly–as if, like* OEDIPUS, *he too could make a proclamation*)

Then hear it, Oedipus! I say that you, unwittingly, live in foul concupiscence with your own blood kin. And you are blind, blind to the evil case in which you find yourself.

OEDIPUS

Do you think you can speak on forever such words as these?

TIRESIAS

If there is strength in truth–

OEDIPUS

There is–but not in you. For you are blind in eye, and ear, and in your soul.

TIRESIAS

(*Suddenly with a cry of pity*)

Oh, you unhappy creature! Defamations you fling at me. But all of them the citizens of Thebes will hurl at you. And soon! Soon!

OEDIPUS

Tiresias, you are the very child of darkness. Night is your mother. But those of us who live in the day's clean light, you cannot harm us ever.

(*Quietly*)

You cannot hurt me or any man.

TIRESIAS

That is true, Oedipus. I cannot hurt you. For by me it is not your fate to fall. But Apollo is the potent agency. It is his business, Oedipus, to bring these things to pass. It is Apollo!

(*There is a pause here of several seconds, with* OEDIPUS *staring at* TIRESIAS *and thinking hard with all his powers of deduction and concentration.*)

OEDIPUS

Ah!

(*He smiles.*)

Creon! So tell me now, are all of these–these insults and inventions–are they yours, or are they Creon's?

TIRESIAS

No, you are wrong, Oedipus. Creon brought none of these calamities upon your head. You yourself upon yourself brought all of them.

OEDIPUS

(*Now believing he has at long last found the key to the mystery*)
Creon!
O wealth, O sovereign power!
O crafts of competition
in the fierce rivalry of life!
What envy is yours, what massive grudge
has been stored up in you
if for this kingship, which the city put
into my hand unsought, a free gift—
If for this, for this, I say,
Creon, Creon most trusted, the state's first friend,
lusted to tumble me out of power,
and, to cover this, suborned a scheming juggler,
this crafty beggar priest,
blind, who has eyes only for gold,
none for his craft.
Am I unjust? Come tell me:
Where were you, clear-sighted prophet,
when the riddling Sphinx was here?
Did you proclaim for Thebes a way of rescue
or salvation? No.
But there was crying need, need for a prophet's skill.
This was no easy oracle
to be unraveled by a—passer-by!
At that crisis you did not show us your wisdom,
either from the augury of birds
or from heaven.
Instead of that, I came,
knowing none of these arts,
I, Oedipus, and quenched the Sphinx,
this through my own intelligence,
not learning how to act from birds!
So here is the man whom you are
trying to hurl from power and,
through Creon's help, stand next the throne.
You think, you and your accomplice,
that with impunity you'll

drive me forth as the polluted man!
If you weren't old and, as I see it, senile,
you'd learn the punishment such traitorous
wisdom deserves!

CHORUS

(*Somewhat in a state of shock*)
Let me say this. The words the prophet has spoken have been angry words. And so have yours, Oedipus. Now we have no need for anger, but only how best to fulfill God's oracle.

TIRESIAS

(*Paying no attention to the* CHORUS'S *speech*)
You are the king, but I, too, in this have power.
I hold the right of speech equal to your own, to
answer fully. I am not your servant, but Apollo's.
I tell you, since you mock my blindness,
that though you have eyes open to the light,
you cannot see the evils all about you;
you cannot see where you live or with whom,
nor do you know from what womb
or from what loins you're sprung.
You are the unwitting enemy of your own kin
living and dead. Cursed by father and by mother,
I tell you a double fury-footed curse
will drive you forth out of this country.
Now you see the light clearly,
but then you will see only darkness.
Yes, and your cry of agony—oh, what
valley or what mountain will not echo it!
And that, soon! Soon!
Then shall you know the meaning of that marriage song
that seemed like a favoring wind
for a fair voyage home,
but it brought you into a disastrous harbor!

Of the other griefs you do not know—
they will equate you in calamity with your true self and with
your children.

And those griefs are without number.
So–you may hurl now your abuse at Creon, if you wish,
or at my mouth, through whom Apollo speaks.
You Oedipus, more than any other mortal man,
will wear out your uprooted soul in wretchedness.

OEDIPUS

How can I endure him! How can my ears listen to this calumny! Haven't you gone? I say that I have turned you out of my house. You are never to return to it!

TIRESIAS

(*Very quietly and slowly*)
I would not have come had you not commanded me.

OEDIPUS

I summoned you–but how could I have known that you had the tongue of a fool!

TIRESIAS

(*Playing on* OEDIPUS' *last word*)
Fool? So in your opinion I am a fool?
(*Pause*)
But to your parents, those persons who brought you to your birth, I seemed wise.

OEDIPUS

(*Quickly*)
Wait! Who were my parents? Who was my father?

TIRESIAS

Today you'll know your birth and be destroyed.

OEDIPUS

So, everything you say is dark, in riddles–

TIRESIAS

Yes, but you are supreme, are you not, in guessing riddles?

OEDIPUS

So you abuse me for the thing in which you found me great?

TIRESIAS

But this greatness of yours—it is that which will destroy you.

OEDIPUS

I do not care—if through that gift I saved the city.

TIRESIAS

(*Terminating the interview*)
So. I am going now. You, boy, lead me away.

OEDIPUS

(*With a final fling*)
Yes, take him away! He's a trouble to me.
Go now, and I'll
blot you from my mind!

TIRESIAS

(*After a few seconds*)
I have spoken the thing which I came to speak. And now I go. But not in fear of your countenance, Oedipus, or of your wrath. You do not have the power to make an end of me. And now I say to you: That man whom you have threatened and long sought, since you made proclamation of search into the murder of Laius, that man I say is here. By report, an alien in our country, he will be shown to be native-born, a Theban, but will not know the meaning of his fortune! Blind he will be, who now has sight, a beggar, who now is rich. Into a foreign land he'll go, tapping the earth before him with his staff. And he will be shown living as brother and father to his own children; to the woman who gave him birth, son and husband; to his father, fellow-sower into the same womb, his mother's; and to his father, son—and murderer. So—go within your palace, think upon these things. And if you find them falsely spoken, then say I have no skill in prophecy.

(*He and the boy go out.* OEDIPUS *returns to the palace.*)

CHORUS

Who has holy Delphi named—
from the temple wrought in rock—

39100

named doer
of deeds unspeakable and
killer with bloody hands?
This is the fugitive's hour,
his instant for fleeing,
but his legs must be swift,
muscled mightier than horses, than
storm steeds in the wind's way.
For leaping and springing upon him
is the son of Zeus,
all armed with the flame of his father,
all armed with the torch of his lightning,
and dreadfully follow,
implacable,
the furies in vengeance.

Oh, the words flame
from snow-capped Parnassus!
Now the oracle is manifest.
Track him down, track him down.
Here, there!
Hunt from his hiding the polluted man!
In rage he rushes
through jungled woodlands,
cowering in caves, over the rocks running
fierce as a bull,
but alone.
O hopeless one, hopelessly fleeing
the holy message which
flows unfailingly
from the earth's navel!
Its words which you
kick with your heels as you fly,
those words are alive;
they will hover and haunt you!

But the brutal utterance
of the master seer
lashes my soul—
I cannot assent,

I cannot deny
this terrible oracle.
I call upon my tongue,
but I am impotent in speech,
for my soul is buffeted
between the tremblings
of despair and hope.
O Apollo,
the past I cannot remember,
the future I cannot see!
Between Corinth
and the house of Labdacus
I have no knowledge of quarreling,
or of any war which Polybus provoked
today or yesterday.
Why, then, should I
in a cause unproven
assault the fair name of Oedipus
before his people,
or avenge the mystery of Laius' death
upon the king?

I know
Zeus and Apollo omniscient
hold in their minds
the destinies of men.
But in this affair
that a mortal seer
can win wisdom greater than mine—
who can perfectly
judge this question?
I know
one man will excel another
in skills of augury,
but till I see
perfect fulfillment of his word,
never will I consent
to reproach the king!
For it shines in my memory

when upon him in those days
came the maiden with vulture's wing
and in the test supreme
his skill was manifest.
Then with what joy
the city hailed him!
So in my heart will I never
impute dishonor to the king.

(*Enter* CREON.)

CREON

My fellow citizens, I have just heard the terrible charge which the king has made against me, and I come to you because his words are intolerable! If in the midst of the city's disaster he believes that I have injured him, by any word or act, I have no wish to live! I cannot live bearing his reproach. For the report strikes at my life—not a part, but all of it! If the state calls me traitor, so will you and all my friends!

CHORUS LEADER

Most probably he spoke the insulting words not in judgment but in anger.

CREON

(*Thinking*)
Someone persuaded the prophet of a falsehood, certainly. Then Oedipus, believing, spoke the words—

CHORUS LEADER

Oedipus spoke the words—I do not know his thought in speaking them.

CREON

When he pronounced the charge against me, was his eye calm? Did he appear wholly sane?

CHORUS LEADER

I cannot say. I never notice the bearing of my masters. But he is coming—through the doors of the palace—Oedipus himself.

(*Enter* OEDIPUS.)

OEDIPUS

You! How did you get here? You with effrontery to face me in my home—proved killer, murderer of the king! And now clear as this daylight, you come to rob me of my crown! By the gods, Creon, what cowardice, what folly did you see in me that made you plot this thing? Was I incompetent to discover a traitor as he crept upon me. Did you think that? Or if I saw him, impotent to defend my life? Yours is a madman's enterprise—to hunt out a kingdom without followers or friends. No, Creon, to seize a throne you need both men and money. So, I find you out both traitor and fool!

CREON

And now you must listen to me—listen as I have to you. When you have heard me out, then judge—

OEDIPUS

Your tongue is clever—and monstrous. I'd be a traitor if I listened to you. But already you're exposed, a trouble-maker and my enemy.

CREON

This very charge which you now make against me—let me tell you—

OEDIPUS

This charge I now make against you—you're a traitor. Don't tell me you are not!

CREON

Stubbornness and stupidity! Oedipus, if you think they prove your case—you're mad.

OEDIPUS

(*Slowly*)

A man cannot turn traitor and escape—because he is a kinsman. If you think that, you are mad.

CREON

I would agree. But tell me now, what wrong have you suffered?

OEDIPUS

(*Choosing his words carefully*)

Did you, or did you not, persuade me to send for the reverend prophet?

CREON

I did. And in such circumstances I would again.

OEDIPUS

(*Thinking*)

When was it, when was it that Laius–

CREON

When Laius what? I cannot read your soul.

OEDIPUS

When he was swept to his death–murdered!

CREON

He died–I'll think back–it was many years ago–

OEDIPUS

Well, at that time was this prophet practicing his craft?

CREON

Oh, yes, with wisdom as great, and as greatly honored as today.

OEDIPUS

Did he make mention of me–in any fashion then?

CREON

No. In any case, not when I was present.

OEDIPUS

You held inquiry into the king's death, at the time?

CREON

We did, of course, but found nothing.

OEDIPUS

Well, at the inquest, I ask you, why didn't this man of wisdom accuse me then?

CREON

I do not know.
(*A pause*)
When in any business I have no knowledge, I am silent.

OEDIPUS

You have knowledge of this business, and could speak out if you would.

CREON

Speak what? I'll not refuse what I know.

OEDIPUS

This! If you had not prompted the prophet, there would have been no calumny which tied me to the king's death.

CREON

You yourself know if the prophet said such things. I must speak for myself. And it is only just, my lord and king, that on the same argument I cross-examine you as you have questioned me.

OEDIPUS

You may ask me questions. But they will not convict me of murder.

CREON

Oedipus, you married my sister, did you not?

OEDIPUS

I cannot deny that.

CREON

You rule the land and give her equal power with yourself?

OEDIPUS

I do, and more. Whatever the queen desires she has from me.

CREON

And I, my lord–for are there not three of us–am I not equal with you both?

OEDIPUS

You are–which makes your treason the more monstrous!

CREON

No! No! Listen to my reasons, Oedipus, as I did to yours! My first point–give your mind to it, my lord. Suppose there are two ways for a man to rule–the one with fear and sleepless nights; the other sweet and calm, without care. Which would he choose? This is my case in all points, Oedipus. I never yearned for a king's name, since I could exercise the substance of power–but without its burdens. I will prove this point to you. Today the whole world wishes me well, and all men hail me in friendship. Why? All who desire some gift of you call upon me first. And so, success with their monarch hangs on me! Why, then, should I seize the throne, when already I have the benefits of sovereignty without its cares. No! In such a case, I say, the man who turns traitor is a fool.

One further point: It is not in my nature, myself to commit the act of treason. And I am too cowardly to join with accomplices in crime. Prove me in this. Go to Delphi, find out if I brought back a true report of what Apollo said. This will testify to my innocence. But if, in any point, you find me plotting with the prophet, arrest and kill me! Yes, kill me then, not on the strength of one voice–but two, your own and mine. But O, my lord and king, do not condemn me privately and in a corner, and on an unproved rumor!

I grant you wrong it is to label traitors lightly as good men, but wrong too to label a good man traitor. For a friend to abandon an honest man is like throwing away what he loves best, his life. My lord, you can only test loyalty over time.

One day is enough to expose a traitor's quality. The righteous man is proven through years of loyalty.

CHORUS LEADER

His words are good, my lord. If you are a prudent man, they may keep you from disaster! Quick decisions, I tell you, are always hazardous.

OEDIPUS

No–if a conspirator plots in quick secrecy, then quickly you must counter him. If I remained calm–and idle–as you counsel me, then the plotter will succeed, and all my cause be lost.

CREON

O Oedipus, what fate do you will for me? Banishment from my country?

OEDIPUS

No. I shall certainly not banish but kill you–to become an example to all who covet kingdoms.

CREON

You yield to no arguments, you give me no faith, you refuse to use your reason–

OEDIPUS

I am using my reason to protect my life.

CREON

O Oedipus, you should use it to protect mine too.

OEDIPUS

But you are a traitor!

CREON

You understand nothing–

OEDIPUS

Whatever I understand, I am king. It is necessary that I rule.

CREON

Not if you rule badly–

OEDIPUS

O city, my city, listen to this traitor!

CREON

Not *your* city, mine too–

(*Enter* JOCASTA.)

CHORUS LEADER

My lords, stop, stop! Now! I see the queen coming toward us from the palace. When she comes, see there are no more arguments before her.

JOCASTA

O foolish and unhappy men–what senseless clamor! Are you not ashamed–with the country in a deathly sickness–to push your private quarrel? Go into the palace, Oedipus, and Creon to your home! You're making a great grief out of nothing.

CREON

Nothing! O my sister–Oedipus threatens me with a double horror. For this choice he offers to drive me into exile from the state, or seize and kill me!

OEDIPUS

That is correctly spoken, my lady. For I have caught him in a vile and treasonable plot against my person and my life.

CREON

No! No! May I lose all hope of life and happiness, and die damned, if I am guilty of this charge!

JOCASTA

In the name of heaven, I beg you to believe him, Oedipus, for his solemn oath, for my sake, and for the sake of these men here who are our witnesses and friends.

CHORUS LEADER

Hear him, my king.
Yield your will and your reason.

OEDIPUS

You wish me to yield–
To what?

CHORUS LEADER

Respect the man whose faith
over the years has never failed–
and who is strong now in his oath.

OEDIPUS

Do you know
what you are trying–

CHORUS LEADER

I know.

OEDIPUS

Well?

CHORUS LEADER

Creon is your friend, and under oath,
and all the evidence against him hearsay.
How then can you accuse him of dishonor?

OEDIPUS

Understand this now and perfectly:
The thing you seek for me–
when you have got it–is my death
or banishment from the country.

CHORUS LEADER

No! And I swear it
by that witness and observer of all things,
the sun, the governor of the gods!
May I die the worst of deaths,

man-hated, god-hated,
if ever I contrived
or held treason in my heart!
I am wretched enough, Oedipus,
seeing our country
blasted by the plague. And now,
if you pile this quarrel upon the old evil,
my heart will burst!

OEDIPUS

(*After a pause in which he stares first at the* CHORUS LEADER, *then at* CREON)
Well, then, let him go! I agree,
even though I surely die,
even though they drive me in exile and dishonor
from the country.
(*Speaking with bitter scorn*)
I am yielding not to his plea for pity,
but to yours. I tell you,
wherever Creon goes, my hate goes with him!

CREON

You are savage when your anger
breaks all bonds–
sullen when you come to yield.
Men with such natures inflict the deepest wounds
upon themselves.

OEDIPUS

Will you leave me and go!

CREON

Now I will go. You have closed your eyes and ears to me,
but these men know me innocent.
(CREON *goes out.*)

(*During the following speeches,* OEDIPUS *stands apart from the* CHORUS LEADER *and* JOCASTA, *nursing his wrath and seeming not to hear.*)

CHORUS LEADER

I believe you should not delay, my lady,
taking him with you into the palace.

JOCASTA

I wish to know what happened.

CHORUS LEADER

Rumors unfounded first aroused suspicion—
then came false charges
to embitter them.

JOCASTA

On both sides?

CHORUS LEADER

Yes.

JOCASTA

But what was the story of treason?

CHORUS LEADER

Since the country is already
in trouble and this quarrel fades,
isn't that enough? Let it alone.

OEDIPUS

(*Shouting*)
See where we are! Though you are a good man,
see where you have taken us, throwing my case away,
trying to blunt my rage—

CHORUS LEADER

I tell you once more, my lord,
I am loyal.
You must surely think me crazed
if in this present crisis I betray you.
I have not forgotten
how,
when this country

was in deep trouble,
you brought us, with a favoring wind,
to safety and salvation.
Today, Oedipus, you are still
our mighty pilot and our guide.

JOCASTA

By the gods, tell me, my lord, what can it be that has put into your heart anger so unquenchable?

OEDIPUS

I will tell you,
for I honor you beyond the protests and opinions of these men.
The root of my rage is Creon and his conspiracy.

JOCASTA

Make it quite clear to me what started this between you two.

OEDIPUS

He says I am the proven murderer of Laius.

JOCASTA

Does he speak as if he knew this himself, or was informed by another?

OEDIPUS

By another. He's brought in the double-dealing prophet to make his charge, which keeps his own lips clean.

JOCASTA

Ah! Then absolve yourself of any anxiety in this business. If you will listen to me, Oedipus, you will learn no mortal has the gift of prophecy. And Tiresias is mortal. I will give you quick and clear proof of what I say. An oracle came to Laius, whether from Apollo himself or from his ministers I do not know–a prophecy that if he and I had a son, Laius was fated to die by that child's hand. Now, Laius was killed by highwaymen at a place where three roads meet. Those were the facts reported. His son, an infant, lived but three short days. Laius fastened the child's ankles with a pin and had him exposed on a deserted mountain. So! Apollo neither brought it about that he kill his father, nor did Laius experience that terrible thing, though he feared it, of being killed by his own son. Such were the prophecies, but I tell you if a god needs to search out anything—like a king's murder—you can be sure he can do it without a prophet's help.

OEDIPUS

What you have said, my lady, stirs to remembrance some deep fear at the bottom of my soul.

JOCASTA

What is it, my lord? What makes you say this?

OEDIPUS

I heard you say—or did I dream it, Jocasta?—that Laius was killed where three roads meet!

JOCASTA

Yes, that was the report, then and now.

OEDIPUS

And the place—where did the tragedy take place?

JOCASTA

Phocis the land is called, and a double road leads to the same spot from Delphi and from Daulia.

OEDIPUS

What was the year when he came to this place?

JOCASTA

Only a little before you appeared and took over the government here; yes, only a little time before that the news of Laius' death was published to the city.

OEDIPUS

O Zeus, what have you so long planned to inflict upon me!

JOCASTA

Oh, tell me, Oedipus, what weighs so deeply on your heart?

OEDIPUS

Do not ask me questions. What was Laius' form and stature? And at that time how old was he?

JOCASTA

A large man, his hair lightly silvered. Not far from your build and stature, my lord.

OEDIPUS

O God! I believe I have already fixed upon my head, in my bleak ignorance, a curse most horrible.

JOCASTA

I am in terror as I look at your face, my lord! What are you saying?

OEDIPUS

I have this terrible fear: The prophet–he may not be blind! But one thing more will tell me most.

JOCASTA

You frighten me. But if I know it, no matter, I will tell you.

OEDIPUS

Did he come with a small escort, or with many soldiers as befits a king?

JOCASTA

There were five in all–among them a herald. And there was a single chariot in which Laius rode.

OEDIPUS

Ah! Ah! It is already shining clear. Now who, who made this report to you, Jocasta?

JOCASTA

An attendant, the only man who escaped with his life.

OEDIPUS

Oh! Does he happen to be with us, here, now?

JOCASTA

No, for from that day when he came home and found Laius dead, and you upon his throne, he took my hand and begged me with tears that I grant the favor he was asking–that I send him far into the country to become a herdsman. So he would be out of men's sight and as far as could be from the city. He was an excellent man–for a slave–deserving a greater gift than this.

OEDIPUS

Could we bring him back at once?

JOCASTA

Of course, but why should you wish it?

OEDIPUS

I am fearful that even now I have spoken too much, my queen. And so I wish to see him face to face.

JOCASTA

Then he shall come. But I, too, my lord–am I not worthy of knowing the troubles in your heart?

OEDIPUS

O Jocasta, I will not deny you, since my mind has gone so far into these byways of terror and of hope. I have had good and evil fortunes, as you know. And to whom but you can I speak out all my heart?

(*Pause*)

My father was Polybus of Corinth; my mother, Merope, Dorian, of noble ancestry. I was accounted eminent, the first citizen of Corinth–until a certain thing happened, an event worth wondering about, but not worth the hot fever it aroused in me. A man who got himself drunk at a banquet shouted from his cups that I was a bastard and not my father's true and rightful son. Furious and tormented, all that day I could scarcely keep my heart from bursting. The next day I went to my father and my mother and questioned them. They were very angry at the man who had let slip the insult, and what they said was a comfort to me. And yet–the story rankled, for it began to spread through the city.

And so, without telling my father or mother, I went to the Pythian oracle. I went to ask the secret of my birth. But to my question Apollo gave me no answer. Instead, he prophesied a thing of horror, saying I was fated to marry my own mother, and bring forth a monstrous progeny for men to see. And this too, that I would murder my own father, who begot me. I listened with all attention, and then I rushed into exile. From that time onward, never have I revisited Corinth, never known my native country again except as a certain spot on the earth's surface under the stars. I went into exile that I might escape fulfillment of the oracle.

And on that journey into exile, I came to the place where you say the king was killed. And now, my lady, I shall speak all truth. When, as I walked, I came near this triple track, there I met, face to face, a herald and a man seated in a horse-drawn chariot, just as you say. The herald in front, leading the way, and the old man also, started to crowd me off the road. I didn't strike the herald, but the driver, who was pushing me, I struck in fury. Then, when the old man saw me do that, he leaned from the carriage and brought a double goad down on my head. He had it in his hand. For that blow he paid a full price. I struck him with my staff, so that he tumbled right out of the carriage into the road. And then I killed them all.

If there be any chance that stranger was King Laius, I am of all men most miserable. Yes, who is more god-hated than I–I who am forbidden to receive into my home any man, stranger, or citizen. It is unlawful to speak with me. Rather, all men are commanded to drive me from their homes. And I, Oedipus, I alone pronounced this curse upon myself. Rightfully, I think. For I defile the marriage of the dead king, with the same hands that killed him! Am I an evil man? O gods, am I not wholly vile! Besides all these things, it is fated that I live always in exile, never again seeing my own home, never again stepping on my native soil. For if I go back to Corinth I must marry my own mother–it is fated–and kill my father, Polybus, who begot me and nurtured me in love. These horrors –perhaps they are a sentence laid upon me by some savage god. Is that the logic of my fate, Jocasta?

No, no, you pure and awful gods, I must never, heaven helping me, see that day. And I say this: Before such stigmata of disaster are fastened upon my head, may I be blotted from the race of mortal men!

CHORUS LEADER

From such horrors I, too, shrink in fear, my lord. But until you question this herdsman face to face, you must have hope.

OEDIPUS

I have hope–just the hope you speak of, and no more–I wait for the herdsman.

JOCASTA

My lord, what is it you are so eager to ask him when he comes?

OEDIPUS

I will tell you. If we find him saying the same thing to me expressly which he said to you–I will have escaped catastrophe.

JOCASTA

I do not understand. What point in the story which you heard from me is so particular?

OEDIPUS

You said this was his report–that robbers, more than one, killed the king. Now, if he reports still the same number, I did not kill him, for many men are not the same as one. But if he should speak of a single traveler, then the evidence weighs against me, and I am guilty of Laius' death.

JOCASTA

Several robbers—that was the report as given. You can be very sure of it. And the peasant can't go back on it. Impossible, for the whole city heard the report, not me alone.

(*After a pause*)

But if he should swerve from his first story, not even then can it be shown that Laius' murder rightly fulfills the oracle. For Apollo expressly said that Laius must die at the hands of my son. Most certainly that child never killed his father. Poor unfortunate, he perished as an infant years before Laius' death. So! Oedipus, for the future pay no attention to prophecies! I would not turn my eyes to right or left for any oracle!

OEDIPUS

You reason well, my lady—and yet, send someone to bring the herdsman, without fail.

JOCASTA

I shall send at once. But now, may we not go into the palace?

(*As they go*)

My lord, you must believe me, in all things I want to do what pleases you.

(OEDIPUS *and* JOCASTA *go together into the palace.*)

CHORUS

May it be my life's fate
to attain that holiness
which is worthiest honor,
in word and in deed,
the foot tracks of whose laws
are printed in heaven,
begotten in the firmament—
their father Olympus.
He only—no mortal—could
beget these statutes;
they are laws everlasting,
oblivion will never take them,

nor will they wax old;
for in them lives the strength of God.

Arrogance out of passion,
arrogance out of pride,
breed always the tyrant.
And swollen in folly
he wins many things
untimely, unprofitable.
To the uttermost ridge he climbs
of power's pinnacle,
and then he plunges sheer
into the abyss of ruin.
Out of that pit
no foot can climb to safety.
So may all tyrants fall.
But I pray the god
never to punish
men who in rivalry fierce
fight for the city's good.
And I proclaim my faith
that the god himself is the city's sovereign.

Oh, if any man walks haughtily
with mocking hand and lip,
and no heart's reverence for the right—
if he dishonors the gods' images
in holy temples—
then for his insolence perverse
may the evil wrath of fate
seize and destroy him!
Or if a man get his profit unjustly,
refrains not
from pollution,
but, profane,
lays hands on the holiest things,
oh, then, amid such infamies,
what man among us may hope
to shield his soul

from the sharp shafts of the god!
If such acts are honored by mankind,
why should I dance–
why should I dance or sing
in worship of the god?

No,
no more will I go to the holy navel
of the earth to honor it,
no more to Abae's temple,
or to Olympia,
unless the prophetic words
fit perfectly the event,
and they be manifest
to all men everywhere.
Now, Zeus, Ruler,
if this name I may cry,
all-mastering god,
let not this blasphemy escape your ear
or be forgotten.
For behold, the ancient oracles of Laius fade,
wiped from the memories of men,
and tarnished is the honor of Apollo. Oh,
the ministries we owe to heaven fade
and faith and worship die.

(JOCASTA *enters carrying a suppliant branch and incense. She starts toward the altar, then turns to face the* CHORUS.)

JOCASTA

Lords of my country, this thought has come to me: I will go to the temples of the gods, with these garlands and incense in my hands. Oedipus has overwrought his spirit with every kind of agony and care. The king cannot distinguish, as a sane man would, between the old oracles and the new, but listens to any man who tells a tale of terror. I have tried to reason with him but have failed. And so I come to you, O Lykian Apollo—your altar is nearest. Here as your suppliant I come, with these symbols of my prayer. Oh, give us release, a happy, safe release from our pollution! Oedipus, the pilot of our ship is shaken with fear—so we are all afraid!

(*She bows her head. Enter* CORINTHIAN MESSENGER.)

CORINTHIAN MESSENGER

My friends, where is the palace of King Oedipus? Can you tell me? Or, better still, where may I find the king himself?

CHORUS

Sir, there is the palace—inside you'll find the king. This lady is Jocasta, his wife and mother of his children.

CORINTHIAN MESSENGER

(*Bowing*)

My lady, how blest you are a queen and mother! May you and your household be forever happy!

JOCASTA

(*With dignity*)

God bless you for this courtesy. And now, sir, why have you come to Thebes, and what have you to tell?

CORINTHIAN MESSENGER

Good news I have—for you and for your husband.

JOCASTA

What kind of news, sir? From what city do you come?

CORINTHIAN MESSENGER

Corinth. And the news I'll tell will please you—surely. It may also grieve.

JOCASTA

What sort of news can have such double power?

CORINTHIAN MESSENGER

The citizens of Corinth will make Oedipus their king.

JOCASTA

What! Does not old Polybus still hold his throne?

CORINTHIAN MESSENGER

No, death holds him now; the king is in his grave.

JOCASTA

(*Excited*)

What are you saying! Is Polybus truly dead, old man?

CORINTHIAN MESSENGER

My lady, if I haven't spoken the truth, why, then–I too deserve to die!

JOCASTA

(*Almost beside herself with relief at the news. She turns to an attendant.*)

Go at once and tell your master. O oracles of heaven, where is your fulfillment now! So long, so long has Oedipus feared and fled this man, that he might not kill him! Now chance, and not the hand of Oedipus, has killed his father!

(*Enter* OEDIPUS *from the palace.*)

OEDIPUS

Jocasta, my beloved wife, why have you sent for me from the palace?

JOCASTA

(*Her eyes shining with triumph*)

Hear this man! And as you hear him, think of the oracles of God. Those holy oracles, where are they now?

OEDIPUS

Who is this man? What has he to say to me?

JOCASTA

He is from Corinth to report–your father, Polybus, is dead.

OEDIPUS

Oh, what are you saying? Sir, tell your message straight to me.

CORINTHIAN MESSENGER

This, then, if it must be told first—and plainly: Polybus is dead—you need not doubt it.

OEDIPUS

(*After a pause of intense thought*)
Ah—was it treachery, or did he die of sickness?

CORINTHIAN MESSENGER

When a man is old, a trifle will tip the scale toward death.

OEDIPUS

O my poor father! He died, then, of disease?

CORINTHIAN MESSENGER

Yes, and because he'd lived a long life.

OEDIPUS

Oh! Oh! My queen, what are we to think now—of the prophetic birds that scream in air? Their voices cried that I would kill my father! But he is dead and in his tomb. I, my sword sheathed, am here, innocent of his blood! Perhaps he died from loneliness, from yearning love for me—and so I killed him? No! Take their plain meaning, and the oracles are false! To Hades, Polybus has taken them, where he, and they, are dead!

JOCASTA

I have long told you this, my lord, this very thing—

OEDIPUS

You have, Jocasta, and yet fears still tug my heart.

JOCASTA

Oh, throw them all away. You must.

OEDIPUS

Surely I must still fear marriage with my mother. Yes, I fear it.

JOCASTA

Oh no! Why should any man have such a fear? Chance rules our lives, and there's no certain seeing what the future holds. It is better to live lightly, from day to day, as best we can. And you, my lord, dismiss this fear from your heart. Many men in dreams have lain with their own mothers. Count all such fears as nothing, so you will easier bear life's burden.

OEDIPUS

All you have said is well said, Jocasta—were she not alive! But I am compelled, though you have reasoned well, to tremble still with fear.

JOCASTA

But this report—the death and burial of your father—is it not for us good news and shining comfort?

OEDIPUS

Good news, I grant, but while she lives, I tremble.

CORINTHIAN MESSENGER

What woman is this who can make you fearful?

OEDIPUS

It is Merope, old man, King Polybus' wife.

CORINTHIAN MESSENGER

What thing about her makes you fearful?

OEDIPUS

A terrible oracle sent from heaven.

CORINTHIAN MESSENGER

Can you tell me the oracle? Or is it unlawful to know?

OEDIPUS

Yes, it can be told. Apollo long ago said I was fated to marry my own mother and take upon my hands my father's blood. For this reason and for many years I have lived far from Corinth. I have been blest by fortune, that is true, and yet it is sweet to a man to look on his own father and mother. This I have been denied.

CORINTHIAN MESSENGER

So, fear of your mother has kept you in exile?

OEDIPUS

(*With a rush of feeling*)

Yes—and not wishing to be my father's murderer!

CORINTHIAN MESSENGER

Then, I will release you from your fear! For I came to do you some kindness if I could.

OEDIPUS

If you did this, sir, you'd richly earn my favor.

CORINTHIAN MESSENGER

For this I came—just so. I thought: well, I may prosper a little when you return as king to Corinth.

OEDIPUS

Never will I revisit Corinth—never look upon my mother's face again!

CORINTHIAN MESSENGER

You have perfected your ignorance in this affair, my son; you do not know what you say or do—

OEDIPUS

I do not? Then, for God's sake, teach me!

CORINTHIAN MESSENGER

Certainly you do not know, if these reasons keep you from your home.

OEDIPUS

Reasons? It is the fear that Apollo's prophecy is true.

CORINTHIAN MESSENGER

And fear that you might defile the woman who gave you birth?

OEDIPUS

Yes! This is the terror plagues me night and day.

CORINTHIAN MESSENGER

Then take my word in full trust: From her you have nothing to fear.

OEDIPUS

How can that be, if I am the child of my own parents!

CORINTHIAN MESSENGER

Because Polybus is nothing to you—

OEDIPUS

What! Was not Polybus my father?

CORINTHIAN MESSENGER

As much your father as I am—as much, no more.

OEDIPUS

You, being nothing to me, how can you be as much my father as Polybus?

CORINTHIAN MESSENGER

Neither of us fathered you is what I mean.

OEDIPUS

If Polybus was not my father, why, then, did he give me hi name? Why did he call me his son?

CORINTHIAN MESSENGER

Listen to me. Long ago Polybus received you as a free gif —from me, from my hands.

OEDIPUS

How could he have loved me so greatly, as he did, if he had received me, as you say, from another?

CORINTHIAN MESSENGER

I'll tell you. Before he took you, an infant from my hands, he had had no children. This was a great grief to him. Do you understand?

OEDIPUS

(*Thinking hard, then harshly*)

Did you buy me, then? Or did you find me in Corinth and give me to him?

CORINTHIAN MESSENGER

I found you in the cleft of a valley in Cithaeron.

OEDIPUS

What were you doing in that region?

CORINTHIAN MESSENGER

I was a shepherd there, in charge of mountain sheep.

OEDIPUS

You traveled about for hire, you mean?

CORINTHIAN MESSENGER

My son, on that day, many years ago, I was your rescuer.

OEDIPUS

Rescuer? What was I suffering from, when you rescued me?

CORINTHIAN MESSENGER

The ankles of your feet will show the trouble you were in, if you will look.

OEDIPUS

O God! Why do you speak of that old grief?

CORINTHIAN MESSENGER

It was I who released you, my son, when a pin bound together those two ankles of yours.

OEDIPUS

I have borne this terrible shame since my infancy!

CORINTHIAN MESSENGER

Of course. The name you bear–

OEDIPUS

By the gods, tell me, was it my mother or my father branded me?

CORINTHIAN MESSENGER

I do not know. The one who gave you to me would know better.

OEDIPUS

You got me from another? You didn't find me?

CORINTHIAN MESSENGER

No, I didn't. Another gave you to me, another shepherd.

OEDIPUS

Who was he? Do you know–can you tell me his name?

CORINTHIAN MESSENGER

He was of Laius' household, they said.

OEDIPUS

Laius who then was King of Thebes?

CORINTHIAN MESSENGER

Yes. This man was one of King Laius' herdsmen.

OEDIPUS

Is the man still living, so I can see him?

CORINTHIAN MESSENGER

(*Turning to the* CHORUS)
Those who live here in Thebes would know better than I.

OEDIPUS

Do any of you who stand near me know the herdsman the man is talking of? Has anyone seen him in the country, or here in the city? Tell me if you have, for it is high time all these things be found out and brought to light.

CHORUS LEADER

I believe he's precisely the man whom just now you've sent for from the fields. But Jocasta, the queen, could better say.

OEDIPUS

My lady, do you know this man whom we have just ordered here? Is he the one the stranger means?

JOCASTA

What man is he talking about? For God's sake, don't listen to him. Do not listen, for what he says is meaningless.

OEDIPUS

Jocasta! With a clue like this I'll never stop this search—until I bring to light the secret of my birth!

JOCASTA

By the gods, no, no! If you love your own life, stop your questioning. Oh, this is all the anguish I can bear!

OEDIPUS

Take heart! Though I am the offspring of slaves—yes, proved a bondsman for three generations, my lady—your honor is untarnished. No one can show you have ignoble ancestry.

JOCASTA

Oh, I beg you, listen to me, Oedipus! Do not do this thing.

OEDIPUS

You cannot argue me out of this search. I will go on to the end.

JOCASTA

And yet, my lord, I am telling you this is best, best!

OEDIPUS

Then, I say this best of yours has far too long afflicted me

JOCASTA

Oh, miserable soul, may you never know who you are!

OEDIPUS

(*Peremptorily*)

Someone go and bring the herdsman here to me. Let the quee rejoice in her noble ancestry.

JOCASTA

Oh, oh, wretched one! For this is the only name I can ca you by—the only name I can ever call you by!

(*She rushes into the palace*)

CHORUS LEADER

Why, why has the queen gone, Oedipus, shaken by the wildes grief? And now no word. I am in terror that a storm of ev will break out of this silence.

OEDIPUS

Let what will break loose! For I tell you, even though I hav the meanest parentage, I wish to know it. Yes, I suspect tha she, like any woman of proud spirit, is ashamed of my birth But I, seeing myself the son of Chance, who has done well b me, I shall not be dishonored. Chance is my mother, and a the months my brothers, marking me at times for humbl things, at times for greatness. I will find out the secret of m birth this day. Having such parentage, how can I be, how ca I ever be other than I am!

CHORUS

Oh Cithaeron, Cithaeron!
If I were wise in skills of prophecy
by heaven, this would be my oracle—
that tomorrow you would know,

unfailingly,
Oedipus' praise of you,
his native land, his nurse, his mother;
and we, too, in summer's festival
would celebrate your honor
in dance and choral song.
This will be most pleasing to our king,
and may it be gracious
in your eyes also, Phoebus Apollo.

My child, my son,
who begot you? Was it Pan,
ranger of mountain crags?
And who of the nymphs immortal
lay in love with your father?
Or was that nymph Apollo's bride?
For all the wildest uplands
are couches for his love.
Was it Hermes who sired you, Oedipus,
sovereign of Cyllene?
Or was it the god of Bacchic frenzy
when he lived on the mountain heights?
With the nymphs of Helicon
he loved most to play.
Was it one of you?
With what surprised delight
he took a newborn son!

OEDIPUS

(*Shading his eyes, looking into the distance*)
I'll make a guess. The herdsman we've sought so long—I've never met him, but I think I see the man. For one thing, he is very old—and my servants are leading him. But your guess would be better—you've seen the man before.

CHORUS LEADER

Yes, and I know him well. He was a herdsman of Laius, and very faithful for a shepherd.

(*Enter the old* HERDSMAN *leaning on a staff.*)

OEDIPUS

(*Turning to the* CORINTHIAN MESSENGER)
I'll ask you first, stranger from Corinth. Is this the man you mean?

CORINTHIAN MESSENGER

This is the man.

OEDIPUS

You, old man, come here. Look at me and answer what I ask. Were you of Laius' household?

HERDSMAN

Yes, and not a bought slave, but raised at home.

OEDIPUS

What kind of work–what was your occupation?

HERDSMAN

For most of my life I tended sheep.

OEDIPUS

In what region chiefly, what places?

HERDSMAN

Cithaeron, and all the land around.

OEDIPUS

Have you seen this man? Do you know him?

HERDSMAN

What? What man do you mean?

OEDIPUS

This man here. Do you know him? Have you been with him ever?

HERDSMAN

I can't say quickly I remember him.

CORINTHIAN MESSENGER

That's not surprising, my lord. I'll jog his memory, for he knows, he knows well when we kept our herds together near Cithaeron. He had two flocks, and I one. We herded them for three years, from March to September. And then in the winter I drove mine to my sheepfolds; he drove his to the stables of King Laius. Am I telling the truth?

HERDSMAN

You tell the truth, but that was a long time ago.

CORINTHIAN MESSENGER

Yes. Well, tell me now, do you remember this—a certain child that you gave me back in those days, that I might bring him up my own?

HERDSMAN

(*Trembling*)
What's that! Why are you asking that?

CORINTHIAN MESSENGER

(*Triumphantly*)
That child you gave me, my friend, is this man here!

HERDSMAN

(*Under his breath*)
Damn you! Will you keep your mouth shut!

OEDIPUS

Stop threatening him! Your words have earned the cursing, not his.

HERDSMAN

(*Cringing*)
O best of masters—how have I done wrong?

OEDIPUS

The child he asks you about—why don't you speak?

HERDSMAN

He talks and talks, but he knows nothing.

OEDIPUS

You! If you won't speak with good grace, I think pain will loosen your tongue.

HERDSMAN

O God! Don't torture an old man!

OEDIPUS

Someone tie his hands behind his back—quickly.

HERDSMAN

For God's sake, why! What more do you want to know?

OEDIPUS

The infant, did you give it to this man, as he says you did?

HERDSMAN

I gave him the child. Would God I had died that day!

OEDIPUS

You will die on this one if you don't tell me the truth.

HERDSMAN

More surely will I die, if I tell. I am lost.

OEDIPUS

(*Looking around at the guards*)
He plays for time—for time.

HERDSMAN

No! I've just said it—I gave him the child.

OEDIPUS

Where did you get it? Was the infant from your own home or another's?

HERDSMAN

It was not my child. It was from another's—

OEDIPUS

From a citizen of Thebes, was it? What family?

HERDSMAN

No, master! For God's sake, ask no more questions!

OEDIPUS

You will die if once more I order you to speak.

HERDSMAN

He belonged—he belonged to the house of Laius.

OEDIPUS

Was he a slave or was he of the family?

HERDSMAN

O God, I am close to telling the horror now!

OEDIPUS

And I to hearing it—but I must hear.

HERDSMAN

It was said to be King Laius' child. But she who is inside—your wife—could better say.

OEDIPUS

She gave it to you, then?

HERDSMAN

Yes. Yes, my lord.

OEDIPUS

Why? For what reason?

HERDSMAN

That I might destroy it.

OEDIPUS

O ruthless, wretched mother!

HERDSMAN

It was from fear of an evil oracle.

OEDIPUS

What oracle?

HERDSMAN

That he would kill his father.

OEDIPUS

Oh why, then, did you give the child to this old man?

HERDSMAN

Pity–I pitied him, my master, and I thought the shepher
would carry him away to his own country. But he has rescue
him only for great evil! O my king, if you are that child o
which he speaks, then from the day of your birth you hav
been accursed!

OEDIPUS

Oh! Oh! All things have come true, all clear, all true! O ligh
of the sun, now for the last time I look on you! For I was ac
cursed in parents and in my birth, cursed in my unholy mar
riage, damned in my father, whom I killed!

(OEDIPUS *rushes into the palace. The* HERDSMAN *and th* CORINTHIAN MESSENGER *go out.*)

CHORUS

O generations of mortal men,
this is how I count you–
living, but not living,
alive, but equal to nothingness.
Who, what mortal being,
wins happiness
or more than an apparition
of glory?
And then the fall abrupt
into oblivion–
Holding you my exemplar,

unhappy Oedipus,
you and your life's destiny,
how can I count any man
under heaven happy?

O Zeus,
it was Oedipus, it was he who,
with excellent skill excelling all,
launched fortune's arrow
to win prosperity
and in all things all happiness.
It was he, Oedipus, who quenched
the riddling Sphinx,
vulture and sorceress,
and for my country stood himself
tower
against death.
Thereafter was he called
to be my lord and king,
honored most,
master in mightiest Thebes.

But now, now, today,
who has heard of creature more wretched
than you? Who has dwelt amid
follies more savage, or endured
agonies more fierce
in life's reversal?
O ample harbor, O marriage chamber
into which entered father, entered son,
O soil your father ploughed,
how could it endure you,
how could it endure you
so long,
and not cry out in shame!

Now, now Time all-seeing
has found you out
in your unwilling sin,

judging late in time
this monstrous marriage,
in which begetter and begotten
were both one.
Would God I had never seen you, Oedipus!
I pour this death dirge from my lips
for myself, for you.
The truth I now speak:
When first I fixed my eyes upon your face
I took into my soul
the breath of life.
Now my eyes close in darkness
and in the sleep of death.

(*A* MESSENGER *enters from the palace.*)

MESSENGER

Elders of our city, honored ever and above all–oh, what things beyond belief you shall see and hear. And if you are loyal still to this house, what sorrow now will seize your soul! For I believe no water that flows can wash clean the evil from these halls: evils now hidden here, but soon to be shown in light of day; evils unknowingly committed, and evils willingly contrived, which bring the doers deepest agony. Oh, both are here and both will be revealed!

CHORUS LEADER

Can anything be added–anything more terrible to the disasters that we know?

MESSENGER

Yes, and to tell in fewest words: Jocasta, the queen, is dead.

CHORUS

O wretched lady! Tell us how she died.

MESSENGER

She did herself to death. You were not there to see the things most grievous. But in my memory they live. So I will tell you as I am able the whole anguish and the end of that unhappy woman.

First she rushed through the palace hall, mastered and maddened by her grief; digging her nails into both cheeks she went into her chamber, straight to that marriage bed of old, and slammed the chamber doors. And then she cried out for Laius long dead–and on the memory of his sowing. How he had died through the son that day begotten! And left her to breed, with Laius' son and hers, a monstrous progeny. So she bemoaned marriage and marriage bed, crying: "Oh, I gave birth to a husband by my husband, and to children by my child!" Then Oedipus burst into the chamber bellowing, and no more could we hear the queen's cries or know her end. Our eyes followed Oedipus as he ranged the hall wildly, begging: "Find me a sword to kill my wife–who is no wife. A double-mother–of Oedipus and of his children." Such were his ravings as he sought her. None of us helped him. It must have been some ghostly guide led him to her chamber. For, like a bull in agony, he bellowed and drove his body at the door. In their sockets the bolts bent backward and he entered, crashing through that double door. And there at last we saw the woman, where she hung, hung swinging, in a noose of twisted cords.

When he saw her, a cry of agony came from him terrible to hear. He loosed the rope which held her and she fell. And when the wretched one lay on the floor, then came the event most horrible of all. Brooches of beaten gold held the dress at her shoulders. He ripped them from the cloth, and then struck hard and full upon the eyeballs of his eyes. "Now you won't see this man again," he cried, "his sorrows or his crimes! Eyes, you will not see her–no, nor my children, which you never should have looked upon! Or ever look on Polybus and Merope, who loved you and whom you longed to see. Forever now you'll look on darkness only!"

Shouting such diatribes against his eyes, he struck again, oh, and again! So in a burst the stream of blood gushed forth and stained his beard. Nor did it cease or slacken, or come drop by drop, but a dark storm of blood beat down like hail upon the ground.

So, now I say, man and woman, here, husband and wife, each of these two suffered their own fates. But more, these evils were commingled, so that each suffered the common horror of the other's fate. Oh, until this hour–no one could argue it–happiness in a full cup was theirs. But now, now, today, and in this single hour–ruin, lamentation, shame, and death. If you can name another evil, it is theirs.

CHORUS LEADER

(*A pause*)
But now? Has the unhappy man some respite from his grief?

(OEDIPUS' *cries are heard from within. The* CHORUS *cannot distinguish the words, but the* MESSENGER, *who stands next to the barred palace doors, makes them out.*)

MESSENGER

He calls on someone to unbolt the doors, and to show to all of Thebes this father-killer, this mother–he speaks the unspeakable. I cannot–then these words: "Hurl me out of the country," he is bellowing. "Let me stay no longer to bring a curse upon my house, the curse which I pronounced with my own mouth!"

(*The cries die down and ebb away in moans.*)

But now his strength fails him, and there is no man to lead or guide him. Oh, now this grief and sickness is more than he can bear. Now Oedipus will show himself to you. For the bolts slide and the palace doors are opening. Soon you will see a sight so hateful that you will turn away in loathing–and yet gaze on in pity.

(*Enter* OEDIPUS *blind.*)

CHORUS LEADER

O tragedy too ghastly for mortal eye!

I have known disasters—
this surpasses all
in horror!
Oedipus, what madness seized you,
what demon sprang—
with a leap unearthly—
into your luckless life,
bringing you pain beyond endurance?
O Oedipus, miserable one,
my heart would ask so much,
but oh, I turn my head—
I cannot look upon your face.

OEDIPUS

O! . . . O! . . .
Ah—wretched am I!
Where does my misery
take me stumbling?
Where is my wild tongue sending these words?
And now, now, O demon god,
where have you leaped?

CHORUS LEADER

Into a place of terror—your own heart.
Where no man may hear or see the god!

OEDIPUS

Darkness!
O horrid cloud
moving upon me—
cloud unspeakable,
cloud implacable—
the breeze blows me
into the harbor of my sorrow.
O God, agony again—
the pin pierces my eyes—
(*After a groan*)
and all my crimes
stab at my heart!

CHORUS LEADER

Oh, it is no marvel, my lord,
that in your doom
a double thrust
strikes at your soul,
and body too.

OEDIPUS

My friend,
my own servant, still steadfast,
faithful!
You outlive them all, still caring
for the blind man!
(*The pain strikes again*)
Oh! Oh!
(*Then*)
You have not forgotten,
and I know you–
even with the darkness I know
your voice!

CHORUS LEADER

My lord, what a desperate deed!
How did you dare it–
to quench your eyes
with darkness?
What god stirred you
to this madness?

OEDIPUS

Apollo–my friends–he
accomplished this evil thing
and all my agony.
But I, it was I alone struck the blow
upon my eyeballs.
Yes, what need have I of them,
since when I had eyes
they looked on nothing good or sweet to see?

CHORUS LEADER

Nothing.

OEDIPUS

O what hereafter might be seen by me,
or loved by me, or heard?
Whose greeting could I still receive with joy?
No! Take me
out of this life as quickly as heaven lets you!
Take me away, my friends,
for I am the lost one, the utterly doomed,
accursed, I say, and of all men
to heaven most hateful!

CHORUS LEADER

Oh, which is most piteous—
your fate,
or this agony of knowledge in your soul?
Would to God I had never known
or loved you, Oedipus!

OEDIPUS

Would God he had died
who saved me on that day—
in the field—
the man who loosed
the fierce shackle from my foot,
snatched me from death!
I do not thank him for my rescue,
for, had I died that day,
I would not be this grievous thing I am,
this misery to friends and to myself.

CHORUS LEADER

Were I to pray,
I too would pray
that death for you.

OEDIPUS

Yes, had I but died, then would I not have been
my father's murderer!
Or called
by everyman

the husband of my mother!
I am godless
and a child of iniquity,
for I entered the marriage bed of my father,
who gave me my own, my miserable life,
and if, and if, I say,
there be other evils
more horrible than these–
then name them,
they belong to Oedipus!

CHORUS LEADER

O my lord, I do not know
how, with right judgment,
I can counsel you,
for you were better dead
than living with those eyes
in blindness quenched.

OEDIPUS

No! No! And do not try to teach me
that this deed done
upon my body and by me
was not well done.
Give me no more counsel!
How, in the region of the dead–
my father walking toward me there–
how could I lift up seeing eyes to his–
or with these eyes ever once more
look upon my wretched mother there!
For what I've done to father and to mother,
hanging is too soft an agony!
To see my children–no!
Born as they were born,
no, not with these eyes.
Or would I have joy
to look upon the city and her towers,
her temples and the statues of her gods–

(*A pause as another memory assails him*)

Oh, from all of these I am cut off—
and by my own decree and curse—
all men must thrust me from their homes,
me, the polluted one,
me, proclaimed by God unholy,
and of the house of Laius!
(*Pause*)
So branded and so cursed, could I gaze upon
any of these things?
No, I'd rather choke the spring of hearing too—
to be both blind and deaf.
That would be sweet—sweet if only the mind
could live beyond the reach
of evil things.

Cithaeron, O Cithaeron, why did you
take me so safely in your arms?
You should have killed me on that instant.
So I would not have blazoned to all men
the secret of my birth!

Polybus, O Polybus and Corinth,
you I believed my country and my home;
there I bloomed as a child,
and you nursed me in youth's beauty—
No, you did not nourish loveliness,
but a cancer,
a poison pulsating in the bud!
Now there is more—
now I am shown to be vile,
the unholy child
of an unholy mother.

O three roadways,
O deep ravine and coppice,
where the way
narrows to a triple track,
you drank my father's blood
spilled by these hands—

do you remember? Do you remember–
and after–when I came to Thebes–what then?

Marriage! O mother–you gave me birth,
and then bore children to your child!
So you created
fathers, brothers, sons, brides, wives, mothers,
working deeds incestuous and monstrous,
and whatever else is shameful in men's eyes!
I cannot speak the word–
for those things which are blasphemous to do,
are blasphemous to name.
Oh, by the gods of heaven, hide me from the sun
as quickly as you can!
Kill me or throw me into the deep–where
the light may never know me!
(*He advances, holding out his hands to the* CHORUS.)
Come!
Come, you may touch this wretched body.
Do not be afraid, my friends,
for you cannot take these evils on yourself–
I, I alone must bear them.

CHORUS

Creon comes–and at a fitting time to act on your request or counsel you. He alone remains and, in your stead, protector of the state.

OEDIPUS

Oh, what can I say! Creon! How, in all justice, can he trust me since he has found me out, but now, his enemy!

(*Enter* CREON *with attendants.*)

CREON

I have not come to mock you, Oedipus, or to reproach you with these evils. They now are past.
(*He walks over to the attendants and speaks to them.*)
If you are not ashamed to exhibit this spectacle of a man polluted before other men, at least respect our lord the sun, whose

blazing light nourishes all of us. I tell you, neither sun nor earth–no, nor rain, which is holy too–will take kindly to such a spectacle. Escort him as quickly as you can into the palace. Only for a kinsman is it decent to look upon another kinsman's agony.

OEDIPUS

Oh–I thank God you did not curse me. Instead, you came in a noble spirit to the vilest of men. So, grant one favor, I beseech you, for your sake.

CREON

What do you beg of me so desperately, Oedipus?

OEDIPUS

This! Throw me out of the country as quickly as God lets you —to some barren land where no man may speak to me again!

CREON

Surely I would have done this. But first–I must know perfectly the god's will.

OEDIPUS

Creon, perfectly the god's word made it clear–that I, the father-killer and the defiled, must die.

CREON

Yes, the oracle–but in this crisis we must search our course most carefully.

OEDIPUS

Creon, though I am a man abandoned by gods and men, will you hear what I have to say?

CREON

Yes, for I know that now you, too, trust in the gods.

OEDIPUS

Creon, this I bid you do–this I beg of you–she who lies dead within the palace, your blood kin, give her burial and all decent rites. As for me, do not condemn the state to death by keeping a living pollution here! Let me go to the mountains in Cithaeron—my Cithaeron, which my father and mother appointed for my doom—there to die the death they willed me. And yet, would death take me there? I do not know.

This I know: Neither disease nor any common thing will cut me off. That day long past I would not have been rescued from murderous death—but that fate held for me some awful end. Whatever that end be, let it go.

My children! Creon, I must speak of them. For my sons I ask nothing of you. Wherever they are, they will find some means to live; they are men. But my girls, my two wretched little girls—they are to be pitied, Creon. I always had them eat at my table. We shared everything. I always loved—I loved my care of them.

Let me touch them now, once, with my hands! And weep at this grievous fate of theirs. Nobly will you do this thing, my lord? If I could touch, I would see! They would be mine!

(CREON'S *attendants lead in the children,* ANTIGONE *and* ISMEME.)

What are these words of mine? O God, I hear my dear ones weeping—my girls. Has Creon pitied and sent them to me? Is this true?

CREON

Yes, it is true, Oedipus. And I have done it because I knew even now you would rejoice in them, as always in the past.

OEDIPUS

God bless you for this joy! I pray God may keep you, Creon —and be a better guardian than he was for me. My children, where are you? Come here to me and to my hands, your father's—and your brother's too—hands which wrought this ruin upon my eyes—which once looked bright upon you.

O my children, I did not know her! No man taught me. How could I know that I would father you—upon the mother who begot me!

Oh, for you I can only weep now—I cannot see you; weep for all the bitter years that will be yours. For all mankind must know this curse. When other women gather, you will not. If to join the city's festivals you go in gladness, you will return in tears.

And when you are marriageable, will anyone dare take this curse upon himself? No. Tell me, is any evil missing here? A father who killed his father; in the womb sowed seed where his own father begot him; brought you into being from the source of his own life! Carrying this load of shamefulness, who then will marry you? No one—all men will cast this in your teeth. Unwedded and in penury you will wear out your lives!

So, son of Menoecius, you are their father now! For we, their parents, are both destroyed—you, their only father. Your kin, do not abandon them to wandering beggary. Do not debase them to my wretchedness. Young and destitute they are of all unless you share and pity them. O Creon, you are noble. Seal for me this promise with your hand.

(CREON *gives him his hand.*)

You children, if you were older and could understand, I'd give you many counsels. But now, do only this—utter this prayer to heaven and say: "O gods, grant this, wherever we are permitted to live upon this earth, may our fate and may our lives be holier and happier than our father's!"

CREON

Oedipus, you have wept enough. Come, we will go into the palace.

OEDIPUS

I must obey, though this and everything is bitter to me now.

CREON

All things done well and in their season are well done, Oedipus.

OEDIPUS

(*In a loud voice, and with a return of his old spirit*)
I obey, but do you know on what condition I obey?

CREON

(*With unexpected gentleness*)
No–how could I know until you tell me, Oedipus?

OEDIPUS

That you send me, that you banish me from this land!

CREON

Ask the gods–only they can grant you this.

OEDIPUS

But I of all men am most hated of heaven!

CREON

Then heaven should quickly grant your wish.

OEDIPUS

Then you agree?

CREON

I do not know heaven's will. Not knowing, I am silent to your question.

OEDIPUS

(*After a pause, in a tone of weariness and resignation*)
So–lead me away and quickly–

CREON

Come, and release these children–

OEDIPUS

(*With a new burst of emotion*)
No! No! Do not tear away my girls–

CREON

Oedipus—you can no longer have your will in all things. Once you lived a life of mastery. That now is finished.

(CREON *and* OEDIPUS *start to walk out slowly.*)

CHORUS

Look upon him, all of you who dwell in Thebes.
Behold, this is Oedipus—he who solved
the riddle of the Sphinx,
and was of all men most masterful.
Upon him fortune smiled, and all men gazed in envy.
Now, now, over him has broken a storm
of terror and disaster.

O you who are mortal, look upon life's end,
and on your own.
Count no man happy until without disaster
he pass the last boundary of his life.

CURTAIN

Oedipus at Colonus

OEDIPUS AT COLONUS

Cast of Characters

OEDIPUS, formerly King of Thebes, now old, blind, and a wandering exile
ANTIGONE, his daughter and faithful guide
STRANGER*
ISMENE, OEDIPUS' other daughter, who after his exile has continued to live at Thebes and is loyal to him
THESEUS, King of Athens, who has jurisdiction over Colonus
CREON, brother-in-law of OEDIPUS and present King of Thebes
POLYNICES, elder son of OEDIPUS and claimant to the throne
MESSENGER
CHORUS of old men of Colonus
CHORUS LEADER
GUARDS and SOLDIERS of CREON
GUARDS and SOLDIERS of THESEUS

Scene: within a grove in the region of Colonus, sacred to the Eumenides, goddesses of the underworld. Center, a rough stone which serves as a bench. Right and to the rear, a ledge of rock. In some modern productions, a statue of a horseman, "The Knight Colonus," is seen in the distance.

(*Enter* OEDIPUS *and* ANTIGONE *from the side.*)

OEDIPUS

Antigone, child of this blind old man,
to what country have we come, what people
live in this town? And who will give a dole

* This is a common term for many characters in Greek plays. Here he is a dweller in Colonus, a stranger to Oedipus and Antigone.

this day to Oedipus, the wanderer?
He asks a pittance—and will receive less.
For me, enough; three things have taught me
to endure: suffering, time, nobility.
But, my child, if you see some seat of rest,
either a public place, or sacred grove,
stop and seat me there; then let us ask
where we are. Being strangers here,
only from the townsfolk must we learn
and do their bidding.

ANTIGONE

O sufferer, Oedipus, my father,
I see tall towers and walls guarding
the city—and not far from here—but
surely this is a sacred shrine and grove
bursting with laurel, grape, and olive trees,
and deep within, so many nightingales
dart to and fro and sing, and sing
their piercing melody. Sit here on this
rough stone. For an old man, what a long journey!

OEDIPUS

Seat me and look after your blind father.

ANTIGONE

Father,
don't teach me the lesson I learned long ago!

OEDIPUS

What is this spot? Where are we resting now?

ANTIGONE

Athens—but this place I do not know.

OEDIPUS

Yes, on our journey, everyone said Athens.

ANTIGONE

Shall I go to ask what place this is?

OEDIPUS

Yes, child, ask if people are living here.

(*Enter* STRANGER.)

ANTIGONE

It is inhabited most certainly.
Now I see a man not far away—

OEDIPUS

Is he coming toward us here?

ANTIGONE

He is here now. You, father, speak to him
the fitting words. I will be silent.

OEDIPUS

My friend, I use this girl's eyes as my own.
You have appeared at just the instant
to explain away our doubts and ignorance.

STRANGER

Before you say a word more, leave this grove.
To walk in holy places is forbidden.

OEDIPUS

What is this place, then? Sacred to what god?

STRANGER

No mortal men live here, for it is holy.
The awesome goddesses possess it,
daughters of Earth and Night—

OEDIPUS

How may I pray to them—by what solemn name?

STRANGER

Hereabouts men call them the All-seeing,
Merciful Ones. Elsewhere they have other names.

OEDIPUS

Oh, mercifully may they receive me, for
I am their suppliant, and from their shrine
and from your country I never will depart.

STRANGER

What do you mean?

OEDIPUS

This place is sign and token of my fate.

STRANGER

Well–I'll not expel you–I'll not presume–
before the city sanctions what I do.

OEDIPUS

By the gods, stranger, I am a wanderer on earth!
Do not deny me what I beg to ask.

STRANGER

Speak. I'll not dishonor what you ask.

OEDIPUS

What, then, is this whole region I have entered?

STRANGER

Listen–and you will learn all that I know.
The neighborhood is sacred to a god.
Divine Poseidon is the owner here,
and in our midst there dwells another god,
the firebringer and titan Prometheus.
The very spot on which you walked is called
the brazen threshold of the underworld,
rampart of Athens. This countryside
boasts as its hero our Knight Colonus,
and all the villagers here in common
do bear his name. All I have told you
is honored less in story than in the hearts
of all who dwell here and who love this place.

OEDIPUS

So, then, the inhabitants are–

STRANGER

Men of Colonus, named for the knight.

OEDIPUS

Does one man govern you or do the people?

STRANGER

Our governor is the King of Athens.

OEDIPUS

What is his name? And is his power
by might or by consent?

STRANGER

He is called Theseus, the son of Aegeus.

OEDIPUS

Could, then, a messenger go to your king from me?

STRANGER

Go with what message and for what purpose?

OEDIPUS

For a small favor done to me,
winning for him a mighty benefit.

STRANGER

What benefit might a blind man do a king?

OEDIPUS

Friend, when I speak, my words will not be blind.

STRANGER

O stranger, I pray you act with prudence
for your own safety, for you are noble,
save for this infirmity you bear. Remain
till I report these things, not to the city

but to our neighbors, for they will decide
whether you are to stay or go.
(*Exit* STRANGER.)

OEDIPUS

O child, has the stranger left us now?

ANTIGONE

He has gone and all is quiet now.
So you may speak, for I alone am here.

OEDIPUS

O dread goddesses, since in your country
and in your sacred grove I first found rest,
be gracious to me now, and to Apollo,
for he it was who, when he prophesied
my life of many ills, added this comfort:
A resting place I should attain at last,
your temple, awful goddesses, a stranger's rest,
here to lay down my worn-out life
and here abiding to bestow benefits
upon my welcomers, and bane on those
who sent and drove me from my home.
If this be truth, grant me some certain sign,
either earth's trembling, or the thunder,
or in the sky God's flaming torch.
For now I know that in my journey here
some inward guide and omen
led me to this grove. Else had I never come
or known, poor pilgrim as I am,
your rites austere, or rested now
upon this rough and sacred stone.
O goddesses, grant me this:
To overthrow my life, to end it here.
Let me pass over and fulfill
Apollo's word. This I beg unless—
unless I am too mean or vile, and have not borne
enough of toils, though bearing more of them
than any man. Come, oh, come, sweet children

of primeval Night–I call on you.
Oh, come, worshipers of Athena. Come,
men of Athens, of all her worshipers
most honored. Come and have pity,
have pity on the ghost of Oedipus.

ANTIGONE

Don't speak aloud. Some old men there
are spying out your seat of rest.

OEDIPUS

I'll be silent, hide myself
in this wood, till we hear
what they say of us.

(OEDIPUS *and* ANTIGONE *move to the side,* CHORUS *enters.*)

CHORUS

(*As they hunt for* OEDIPUS *in the sacred grove*)
Look! Who was that? Where is he hiding?
Shameless, insolent!
Now he has run off–
Look closely now,
we must search everywhere.
(*They catch sight of* OEDIPUS.)
Ah, he's a tramp,
an old vagrant, and a foreigner.
No native of Attica, no native
would have stepped foot
within the holy grove
of our ladies implacable!
We are afraid to speak there,
turn our heads when we pass,
reverent and speechless.
We only utter the prayer in our thoughts
as we pass by–
Now, I've hunted the sacred wood
all over,
I can't find where he's hiding.

OEDIPUS

(*Appearing*)
I am here–
A blind man,
I see you with my ears.

CHORUS

Oh! Oh!
He is terrible to see!
He is dreadful to hear!

OEDIPUS

I beg you–I am a suppliant
and not lawless–

CHORUS

O God, protect us–
Who is this old man?

OEDIPUS

O men of Attica,
as you see I am not one
favored by fortune,
else I had hardly
used another's eyes to guide me here.
You see me, a man, led by a child.

CHORUS

Ah–were you born with this blindness?
I can see you have lived long
in wretchedness. But I won't have you
add to your miseries
with curses. They will fall upon you
from your trespass here,
for this grove is holy.
We pour libations here
in this green dell–
cups of fresh water
and then with honey mixed.
We won't have you stumbling about

where no man may go or speak.
Now, away with you! Out of here!
Do you hear, blind, wretched creature?
If you have more to say,
go first from this holy ground,
then you may speak.
But first go!

OEDIPUS

Daughter, what in heaven's name can we do?

ANTIGONE

We must yield, father, obey
the customs here.

OEDIPUS

Take my hand.

ANTIGONE

Here.

OEDIPUS

O strangers—
if I, consenting, go from this place
in trust—do not betray me!

CHORUS LEADER

(*Pointing*)
Those seats there—we won't expel you.

OEDIPUS

Is this far enough?

CHORUS LEADER

No, beyond—

OEDIPUS

(*Moving slowly*)
More?

CHORUS LEADER

Child, you understand–lead him further.

ANTIGONE

Come where I take you, father.

CHORUS LEADER

Man of misery,
you are a stranger in a strange land–
so you must obey us,
hate what our city hates and
reverence what it loves.

OEDIPUS

Come, child, lead me–
yes, into their paths of reverence–
so we won't set ourselves
against these rules
or speak what is forbidden.

CHORUS LEADER

Here. No, not beyond this ledge.

OEDIPUS

This way?

CHORUS LEADER

Yes, enough.

OEDIPUS

Shall I sit down?

CHORUS LEADER

Yes, to one side, on the edge of the rock.

ANTIGONE

Father, this is for me to do–
Now easily.

OEDIPUS

(*In pain of body and spirit*)
Oh! Oh!

ANTIGONE

Your steps—keep them by mine—lean—

OEDIPUS

O God, I suffer!

CHORUS LEADER

Miserable man—
When you are comfortable
and released from your pain,
then speak to us.
Who are you, great sufferer?
Who brought you here?
And what is your country?
Yes, I must examine you.

OEDIPUS

O stranger, I have no country!
Do not—

CHORUS LEADER

You hold back something from us.
What?

OEDIPUS

Oh, do not ask me who I am—
or torture me with questions.

CHORUS LEADER

What are you saying?

OEDIPUS

My birth—a thing of horror—

CHORUS LEADER

Speak!

OEDIPUS

Child, what in God's name do I say?

CHORUS LEADER

And what is your family—your homeland?

OEDIPUS

What will happen to me, my child?

ANTIGONE

Speak now—you must.

OEDIPUS

The end! I will speak—

CHORUS LEADER

Then quickly—you've hung back too long.

OEDIPUS

You know the race of Labdacus?

CHORUS LEADER

O Zeus!

OEDIPUS

Of Oedipus, the wretched?

CHORUS LEADER

(*Shuddering*)
Yes—are you he?

OEDIPUS

You must not be afraid
of what I speak.

CHORUS LEADER

O God!

OEDIPUS

They will not listen—I am lost!

CHORUS LEADER

Oh! Oh!

OEDIPUS

Daughter–what will it be now?

CHORUS LEADER

You must leave the country–
You must leave! Go! Go!

OEDIPUS

But your promise!
Fulfill what you promised me–
You must!

CHORUS LEADER

You deceived us,
hiding your name! So
it is no crime
to pay you for that,
not with a gracious gift–
but with a painful penalty!
Get off those ledges, go!
Yes, out of this land–
I will not have
pollution infect the city.

ANTIGONE

O strangers,
if you refuse to hear my father,
the old wanderer, blind,
telling his unwilling deeds,
then hear and pity me,
a woman in misery
who prays you for her father's sake,
for his sake only.
I turn eyes not blind upon your face.
Think of me as you would
a kinswoman come to entreat
pity and respect

for this wretched man.
Oh, we are the suffering ones!
And as in God's hands
we are in yours!
Oh, come,
nodding your head,
surprise us with your graciousness!
I beg you, I beseech you
by whatever is most dear–
your child, your wife, your heart's desire,
or things divine–
Oh, have pity upon us,
for surely you must know
no man, God leading him,
escapes his doom.

CHORUS LEADER

O child of Oedipus,
we pity you and him
for your misfortune and for his.
But before the oracles from heaven
we tremble. We can say no more.

OEDIPUS

How empty, then, is Athens' glory,
her fair repute dissolves into thin air!
All men have boasted she was foremost
amongst all cities honoring the gods,
first in power to rescue and defend
the abused stranger.
But you, how have you been Athenians to me?
Routed from my seat, then driven away,
driven from fear, fear of my name only, for
you cannot fear my person or my deeds,
deeds which were suffered, not committed.
If of my mother I must speak and of
my father–there lies your fear, I know,
come, tell me
how in my soul am I an evil man?
I fought against my killers, blow for blow,

not knowing. But had I known, no man
for that encounter could hold me guilty.
Both father and mother I came upon
unknowingly. But when I was a child
they planned my death. They knew, they knew!
Now, by the gods whose suppliant I am,
and in whose name you routed me—
restore my safety now as you have pledged.
Don't think to worship in one breath,
denying in the next the rites you owe.
No mortal creature escapes his doom,
for the eye of heaven knows full well
who are the god-fearing, who the godless men.
Do you suppose your blasphemous acts
do please the goddesses? You only
tarnish the fair name and fame of Athens, for
as her suppliant you took me in
and made your promises, so save me now and
guard me from all perils. Now as you gaze
upon this ruined face, do not dishonor it.
I bring a blessing to all dwellers here,
and when your ruler comes, whoever
he may be, listen, you will learn all. Till then
do me no evil.

CHORUS LEADER

These words out of your heart
I fear and reverence.
They are heavy with authority
and gravely spoken. I am content
to wait the judgment of the king.

OEDIPUS

Who, my friends, governs this region here?

CHORUS LEADER

The King of Athens, holding his father's throne,
and the same courier who sent me here
will now conduct the coming of the king.

OEDIPUS

But a king, would he respect a blindman?
Why should he concern himself with me or come?

CHORUS LEADER

He'll come, most surely, when he hears your name.

OEDIPUS

My name? Who will have told him that?

CHORUS LEADER

The lips of many travelers, for the road
to Athens is wide and words fly fast.
Be very sure, the king will hear and come.
Old man, the name of Oedipus has swept
throughout the world. And though he be asleep,
he will arouse himself and come with speed.

OEDIPUS

Oh, then,
may blessings fall upon this city and on me!
Most favors paid pay back the donor too.

ANTIGONE

O Zeus! My father, what can I say or think?

OEDIPUS

What is it, Antigone?

ANTIGONE

I see a woman coming nearer, nearer—
riding a Sicilian colt—wearing a sun hat—
the broad brim hides her face. What shall I say?
Yes, she! No, it is not—my brain is dizzy—
it can be no one else! Her eyes are smiling now
upon me as she comes. Ismene!

OEDIPUS

What are you saying, child?

ANTIGONE

Your daughter and my sister. One moment
she will speak and we will know.

(*Enter* ISMENE.)

ISMENE

O voices dearest to me–
my father's and my sister's–
at last I've found you, but with pain and tears.
Now as I see you I must weep again.

OEDIPUS

Child, you have come–

ISMENE

O father–
your doomed life–
I see it now with my own eyes.

OEDIPUS

You have really come!

ISMENE

And not without grief and hardship.

OEDIPUS

Touch me, child.

ISMENE

My arms about you both.

OEDIPUS

My own!

ISMENE

Oh, what lives of misery you lead!

OEDIPUS

Mine and your sister's, yes.

ISMENE

Oh, and mine too!

OEDIPUS

Child, why have you come?

ISMENE

Thinking of you, I–

OEDIPUS

You longed for me?

ISMENE

I've made myself your courier, father.
In Thebes I only am your faithful follower.

OEDIPUS

But the young men, my sons, where are they?

ISMENE

Where are they?
Oh, now the news is fearful to report.

OEDIPUS

Those two! In nature and in way of life
they are Egyptians! In Egypt men by custom
sit indoors at weaving frames; the women
go out of doors and earn the daily bread.
Like you, who do your brothers' part, while they
remain at home like girls. You two
share with me my miseries–not they.
Antigone, from the time she ceased to need
a child's nurture and had her body's strength,
has been companion to my wanderings.
Yes, forced by fate to be an old man's guide
in the wild woods, often without food,
roaming barefoot, daring to endure
the heavy rains or burning rays of sun.

At home there was food, luxury,
but she thought only of her father's care.
Ismene, once before you came
bringing me secret oracles of my fate.
Yes, and when I was driven from the city
you were faithful. So, now what word
do you bring, Ismene, to your father?
What is this journey's mission, for I know
you have a message, if only terrors, to report.

ISMENE

My own father, the sufferings I bore,
seeking to find you–how you lived and where–
I'll leave unspoken. To speak of those
would be to suffer twice my journey's pain.
But to tell all the evils that cleave still
to your ill-fated sons I've come to you!
In the first years both sons were mindful
of the old blight still clinging to your name.
So willingly they left your throne to Creon.
But now both are obsessed! A rivalry,
fiendish, infatuate, enters their hearts
to seize your power and kingdom, each for himself.
Your younger son has stripped the elder
of royal rights and driven him from Thebes.
Your elder, Polynices–this is the report
at home–has gone to Argos for his exile,
there, by a new high marriage,
won for himself confederates and allies.
So Argos and Thebes–and soon, they say–
will win great glory battling with one another,
Argos if she conquers Thebes with honor,
and Thebes if Argos fails and falls before her.
O my father, these are not wild words
or rumors–all are true, all terrible!
One day I know the gods will show compassion
upon your sufferings, but when,
oh, when, I cannot tell.

OEDIPUS

And yet, Ismene, your last words stir some faint hope in me.
Someday—

ISMENE

Father, I come with new words of prophecy.

OEDIPUS

What is the oracle, oh, tell me, child?

ISMENE

Whether you live or die, my father, men
will seek you out—and soon—for the good luck,
for the good fortune you can bring.

OEDIPUS

How can good fortune spring from such a man as I?

ISMENE

The power to rule, or to win wars,
which your sons seek, lies in your hands.
This is the report.

OEDIPUS

What! When I am nobody, suddenly
I become a man.

ISMENE

Once the gods sought to destroy you, father.
Now they would lift and exalt you.

OEDIPUS

What a trifling miracle for the gods
to bring to pass.

ISMENE

Know, father, on account of this trifle
Creon comes to Athens soon.

OEDIPUS

Creon? To do what? Explain.

ISMENE

To bring you into Theban hands—
not into the town, but beyond the gate.

OEDIPUS

Beyond the gate? What use would I be there?

ISMENE

Your grave, when you die, if men dishonor it
the gods will punish them.

OEDIPUS

Ismene, it takes no oracle to tell me that.

ISMENE

And so they want you near Thebes and fully
in their grip.

OEDIPUS

But when I die, they will bury me, Ismene,
in Theban soil?

ISMENE

Oh no, they say that blood guilt
prevents your burial in Thebes.

OEDIPUS

Ah! then, never will my sons or Creon
lay their mastering hands on me!

ISMENE

Then will misfortune fall upon the city.
The time will come.

OEDIPUS

What are you saying? What do you mean?

ISMENE

When Theban armies enter Athens
they will fall in battle at your grave.
Your angry spirit—

OEDIPUS

Who told you what you are telling me, my child?

ISMENE

The embassy from Delphi–from the oracle.

OEDIPUS

These things which touch me and my fate,
Apollo spoke them?

ISMENE

When the embassy came from Delphi,
this they reported.

OEDIPUS

Did my two sons hear them?

ISMENE

Both sons–and understood them well.

OEDIPUS

Ah! and those fiends, hearing them,
thought only of the kingdom for themselves,
not of me or my desires. Is that the truth?

ISMENE

It breaks my heart that you must say it.
It is true.

OEDIPUS

Then may the gods not quench their fated
quarrel with one another, but let me at the last
be arbiter in this war they have brought
upon themselves. And let this be the issue–
that neither the one who holds my throne
and scepter, nor the exiled one who comes
again to Thebes, will ever rule.
They left me, their father, helpless at home,
then shamelessly thrust me out,
driving me from Thebes, and publicly

proclaimed my banishment. Don't tell me
that exile was my wish, a boon granted
by the city. No! Years before, when passion held me
when I most longed to die–
even to be stoned with stones–then no one
helped me or fulfilled my wish.
But after, long after, when suffering had eased,
when I knew passion had run its course,
when I knew
chastisement was greater than my sin–
then, oh, then, the city with violence
drove me from the land, my sons
consenting and accomplices, my own sons
unwilling to act, though able. So I became
a beggar for want of one word from them,
an exile and a wanderer as I am today.
But, my friends, from these two, though born as women,
I get my livelihood, such safety as
I anywhere enjoy, and the dear services
of kinswomen. But my sons–they tore from me
my throne, my scepter and my kinsmen!
Neither will get me as ally
and never will Thebes bless their rule.
This I know now, for I have
heard from you, Ismene, this new oracle,
and the old one, given to me by Apollo,
has been fulfilled. Add to this
what you have told me: They are sending Creon–
or some other–to search me out!
O my friends, if you would do the will
of these dread deities, guardians
of this place, then you will win salvation
for the city and vengeance on my enemies.

CHORUS LEADER

Worthy you are of our compassion,
you and your children, Oedipus. And now, besides,
for our protection, you would give yourself!
So in my turn and for your safety
I wish to give you counsel–

OEDIPUS

My friend,
be my guardian. Speak, I will obey.

CHORUS LEADER

First make atonement to the goddesses
for the trespass when you entered here.

OEDIPUS

How shall I perform it? Teach me, my friend.

CHORUS LEADER

Bring holy offerings from the fresh spring.
Do this with hands washed fresh and clean.

OEDIPUS

And when I have brought the clear libation?

CHORUS LEADER

There are bowls here, wrought with great beauty.
Wreathe their brims and their two handles.

OEDIPUS

With olive? Or with tufts of wool, and how?

CHORUS LEADER

You take the fleece of a ewe lamb for this.

OEDIPUS

Yes. And how must I complete the rite?

CHORUS LEADER

Stand and pour, facing the eastern sky.

OEDIPUS

And with those bowls you speak of will I pour?

CHORUS LEADER

Pour the draft from three, emptying the last.

OEDIPUS

Tell me—I have filled the bowls with what?

CHORUS LEADER

With water and with honey. Bring no wine.

OEDIPUS

When the dark earth receives the offering?

CHORUS LEADER

Upon that place put olive branches—
And how many? Three times nine, using both hands.
As you arrange them, let this be your prayer—

OEDIPUS

The prayer beyond all else I long to hear.

CHORUS LEADER

Our goddesses we call Merciful Ones.
So ask them to receive their suppliant
to gentle breasts. You yourself must make
this supplication for your safety—yes, and
for ours—you or someone speaking in your stead.
Let not the voice be lifted, inwardly
utter the prayer. Then go and never,
never turn back your head, but go at once.
If all these ritual acts you do, take heart,
I stand your guardian. If you reject them
I tremble for your safety.

OEDIPUS

O children, you have heard these words from those
who dwell here and who know these rites.

ANTIGONE

We have. Instruct us what we should do.

OEDIPUS

Friend, for myself I can perform nothing,
having a twofold infirmity—
no strength of body, no eyes to see.
So may not one of these perform the rite?
I believe one soul may make atonement

for many sins—if she be pure in mind.
But let it be done quickly—and so
I won't be long abandoned.
For when alone
I am strengthless. I cannot even walk
without a guide.

ISMENE

I go—and I will perform this rite.
But now, how may I seek out the place?

CHORUS LEADER

Within this grove. It is but over there.
If you need further guidance, there the keeper
of the shrine will teach you all.

ISMENE

So, then, I go. You stay, Antigone. Care
for our father. We are daughters—
Whatever the burdens we must carry them.

CHORUS LEADER

Terrible it is, I know,
to rouse the sleeping memories
of an old evil,
but I wish to question you.

OEDIPUS

What's that? What's that?

CHORUS LEADER

Yes,
speak to me
of that horror, and that pain
from which you have no pathway
of escape.

OEDIPUS

Oh, no!
No! By my guest rights

in your country,
do not open to the world
these shames I have suffered.

CHORUS LEADER

I desire from you
thc full, the honest story,
holding nothing back.

OEDIPUS

O God!

CHORUS LEADER

Yield, I beg.

OEDIPUS

Oh! Oh!

CHORUS LEADER

Yield to me–I granted your petition.

OEDIPUS

In my innocence I have suffered–
not committed–
evils most fiendish.
The gods be my witness!
The city caught me
in an evil marriage
which was my fate.

CHORUS LEADER

I heard the story–
You entered the bed ill-omened
of your mother.

OEDIPUS

O death! It is like death to me
to hear your words. Yes,
these two I have begotten–

CHORUS LEADER

What are you saying?

OEDIPUS

My two girls, my fates–

CHORUS LEADER

O Zeus!

OEDIPUS

Travail of one mother gave us birth.

CHORUS LEADER

These are your children–and–

OEDIPUS

Their father's sisters–

CHORUS LEADER

God!

OEDIPUS

Blow upon blow of horrid evil!

CHORUS LEADER

You suffered–

OEDIPUS

I bore what cannot be borne!

CHORUS LEADER

Crimes–

OEDIPUS

No.

CHORUS LEADER

What?

OEDIPUS

A prize for saving the city
this accursed marriage.
Would God I had never won it!

CHORUS LEADER

Wretched man! But
you committed murder–

OEDIPUS

What's that?

CHORUS LEADER

You killed your father–

OEDIPUS

You flog me again!
You flog my wounds!

CHORUS LEADER

But you killed–

OEDIPUS

I killed–but–

CHORUS LEADER

What?

OEDIPUS

I will tell you. The men I killed attacked me to kill.
Unknowing I came upon them. I am innocent of the crime.

CHORUS LEADER

Ah now, Theseus has come, our king,
the son of Aegeus, and at your bidding, Oedipus.

(*Enter* THESEUS *with* GUARDS.)

THESEUS

O Oedipus,
over the years I have heard many speak
of the bloody work you wrought upon your eyes–
so would I have known you, son of Laius–

and now, upon my journeying here,
I learn more deeply of your life and fate.
'Till now—this dress—oh, and your ruined head—
show me in truth that you are Oedipus.
You have my pity. But I long to ask
what are your petitions
that bring you to this city and to me,
you and this comrade in your misery?
Come, tell me, for whatever history
of deep disaster you unfold to me
I will have lived and known it.
I, too, was schooled in exile and alone,
enduring long in foreign lands
a thousand perils to my head.
So, heaven help me, I would not turn my hand
upon a stranger, save to succor him.
Being mortal, this I know—
only an interval of time divides
your nothingness today from mine tomorrow.

OEDIPUS

O Theseus, your nobility breathes in these words,
though they are brief and few. And so will be my answer.
You have told my name, my father's too,
and Thebes, my native land. So what remains to tell?
Only what I desire of you. Then we are done.

THESEUS

Tell me at once so I may fully know.

OEDIPUS

I have potent powers which can bestow
a gift upon you—my wretched limbs and frame.
Not beautiful to look upon, but more
than a fine body are its benefits.

THESEUS

And you believe it brings
what kind of benefits?

OEDIPUS

That you will later learn, not now.

THESEUS

But when—when will these gifts be manifest?

OEDIPUS

When I am dead and you have buried me.

THESEUS

So only for your life's ending do you
petition me? But what of all things between
your death and now? Have you forgotten them?
Or do they mean nothing?

OEDIPUS

At the time I die all things will be given me.

THESEUS

What you ask now is a slight gift.

OEDIPUS

No. Consider well this gift. Not slight,
for mighty issues hang upon it.

THESEUS

You mean a struggle with your sons—
They will deny my right to keep you here?

OEDIPUS

Theseus, my sons would bring me back to Thebes.

THESEUS

But you are willing surely? Exile is no happiness.

OEDIPUS

No, I am not willing, for when I longed,
I deeply longed for Thebes, they banished me.

THESEUS

O foolish man—this anger will not cure your ills.

OEDIPUS

When you know all, you may rebuke me.
Until then, no!

THESEUS

Teach me, Oedipus. Without knowing—
and from your own lips I have no right to speak.

OEDIPUS

I have suffered an evil—piled on many more.

THESEUS

The ancient curse upon your house—

OEDIPUS

No. Long, long all Greece has known
that curse and agonized.

THESEUS

But what grief greater for a man to bear?

OEDIPUS

I was driven out of Thebes, my home.
By whom? By my own sons!
And now, father-killer as I am,
I never can return.

THESEUS

I do not understand. If it is fated
and forbidden for you to live in Thebes,
why do your sons send to bring you home?

OEDIPUS

An oracle has spoken—and fear drives my sons.

THESEUS

What oracle? Tell me this fear.

OEDIPUS

Unless they have my body they are doomed
to die in battle here.

THESEUS

But how could that be? We are not enemies,
nor is there any bitterness between
your state and ours.

OEDIPUS

O son of Aegeus, O my friend,
this you must know: It is only
the deathless gods who age not
nor ever die. The whole world else
all-conquering time confounds; the might
of earth, the body's strength decays.
Yes, faith dies, and budding faithlessness is born.
Never do men or cities hold enduring love
for one another, but with each tomorrow
joy turns to bitterness. Then, with a
day's passing, grows again in love.
So this I say: If today Thebes smiles on you,
oh, then, tomorrow
time, mother of measureless days,
will from her womb bring forth that bitter word
to shatter all your covenants
in bloody war.
And then my cold corpse, sleeping in the earth,
will drink their warm blood streaming.
All this will come
if Zeus be Zeus and if his son speaks true.
But I must not profane such mysteries
with speech. Let me end where I began:
You will be blessed if but you do your part
as I do mine. Unless the gods are lying to us both.
No, I tell you, you will never say
of Oedipus: What an ungrateful guest and citizen
I welcomed to this state!

CHORUS LEADER

My king, the stranger's promises
made many times–surely he will
bring these things to pass.

THESEUS

And who could reject such grace
from such a man! First the rights of a spear friend
and an ally are due him. Then, too, he comes
a suppliant to our gods. And third,
no small blessing he will bestow
in recompense. All this I reverence–I
take his gift. And now I establish you
a member of this state and city.
If you wish to abide in this region,
I order your protection here. If to go
with me is your wish, Oedipus,
I promise you the choice is yours alone.

OEDIPUS

O Zeus, I pray–with your goodness
favor such men as these.

THESEUS

So tell me your desire. Would you come
to live in my home with me?

OEDIPUS

If fate permits it– No, this is the place.

THESEUS

To do what here? I'll not oppose you–

OEDIPUS

Here I will master those who drove me forth.

THESEUS

You argue strongly.

OEDIPUS

Yes, if your word and promise are fulfilled.

THESEUS

Have faith, I'll not betray you.

OEDIPUS

I believe and ask no oath.

THESEUS

My word is enough.

OEDIPUS

But to protect me, what will you do?

THESEUS

Fear grips you. Why?

OEDIPUS

Men will come to take me—

THESEUS

(*Pointing to his* GUARDS)
This will be their business—

OEDIPUS

But you leave me, and you must—

THESEUS

Don't tell me what I must or must not do!

OEDIPUS

Fear makes me press you—

THESEUS

But in me there is no fear—

OEDIPUS

The threats—you do not know them.

THESEUS

This I do know. No man will take you from me
by violence. Look–many men mouth many threats
in folly or in anger. But if I am the master of my soul,
all threats dissolve in air. Those braggarts
from Thebes may have screwed their courage up
to threaten you with capture. But
there is a broad sea–and rough to cross–
between that place and you. Take heart.
I remind you, even without my promises
you have Apollo's word who sent you here.
Besides, even were I to go,
my name alone will shield
and guard you here.

(THESEUS *and* GUARDS *go out.*)

CHORUS

Stranger, to a land
glorious in horse and horsemen,
earth's fairest home,
to shining Colonus, you have come!
For here the nightingale
sings oftenest and best,
sings sweet,
more piercing sweet and clear
under our green hill's covert.
And here the ivy grows
with clustering berries climbing,
dark, deep dark as is his wine,
for this is Bacchus' bower
inviolate. And here
no sun may scorch,
no wind can blow,
nor any winter's storm.
But here the Ecstatic One
forever walks,
Lord Dionysus,
with his girls divine
who tend and follow him.

Here, here,
fed by the dew of heaven,
blooms the narcissus in our earth
and weaves in lovely clusters,
morn by morn,
the antique crowns of Demeter
and her child.
Here, too, the crocus gleams,
lighting its golden ray;
nor do these fountains sleep
or fail to feed Cephisus, that river wanderer,
but, day by day and forever,
their pure and potent water brings
birth to the folding plain,
swift birth to the breasting earth.
In such a land
the Muses do not scorn
to dance or sing,
nor fails the grace of Aphrodite
with her reins of gold.

A tree grows here
unplanted in the soil by mortal hand,
unconquerable
and self-begotten.
Never in Asia has it grown as here,
nor in the mighty isle
of Dorian Pelops;
but from this earth,
a terror to our enemies, it springs.
Here in this land,
where it blooms best,
behold,
immortal in our earth,
the gray-green, child-nurturing
olive tree!
Not youth's rash hand
nor grip of grizzled age
can blast or wither it.

But watchful Athena, gray-eyed,
and Morian Zeus with his encircling eye
guard it forever.

Another story of glorious praise,
your pride and the highest,
O Mother City, I must tell–
gift of the mighty god,
gift of the Lord Poseidon;
for you have clothed her,
O Son of Cronos,
with power and double glory–
the mastery of horse and rider,
mastery and might of the sea.
Here first in Colonus' roadways
wild horses were curbed and were broken,
tamed to the bit and the bridle.
Here first came the skill of the oarsmen,
and the fleet ships leaping
over the wonderful, over the terrible sea,
while feet of a hundred Nereids
danced in the foam that follows.

ANTIGONE

O land most blest with praise–
now you must show in deeds for us
these shining words.

OEDIPUS

Child, what is happening now?

ANTIGONE

Creon–he comes, he comes,
and not without pomp and escort.

OEDIPUS

Dear friends and elders of this land,
it is over–the safety and the refuge
which you gave is finished.

CHORUS LEADER

Take heart, not finished. Though I grow old,
this country's strength is young.

(*Enter* CREON *with* GUARDS *and* SOLDIERS.)

CREON

O noble citizens of Athens—
suspicion—I find it written in your eyes
upon my coming. Oh, have no fear of me,
and let your greetings be in friendship.
I come an old man—no conspirator.
I know the majesty of Athens and its might
in Greece. Oh, no! A gray-headed ambassador
I come to ask and urge this old man here
to follow me. For that I have a mandate
from all of Thebes. And of our citizens
I of them all most deeply feel his wrongs.
Now—most unhappy Oedipus, hear me
and come home! For all the Theban people
summon you—I more than any other—for
would not all men despise me
did I not grieve more deeply for your wrongs?
Seeing you now in exile and in wretchedness—
a wanderer ever, leaning upon one handmaid,
one only for life and livelihood,
walking in want and penury. Oh, and she—
what a wretch I am! For never did I dream
that she would fall so far, unhappy girl,
as ever to be your nurse and guide,
living a beggar, unwedded, young—
a prize for ravishing by the first comer!
What a deep reproach to me, to all my kinsmen.
Yet all this shame, Oedipus, has not
been hidden. By your fathers' gods, it's you
must hide it now! So yield to me, come home
to the city which is yours. Give Athens
your grace and gratitude. But Thebes
nurtured you— Come home.

OEDIPUS

So you weave, O arrogant one,
out of right reasons this slippery net!
Why do you lust again to seize me a second time
your prisoner, when it will torture me the most!
Before–
when my soul was sick with horror
and with suffering–to have been cast out
would have been happiness– But no–then you denied me.
But after–
when my rage and passion had fulfilled themselves
and when living at home would have given
sweetness and balm to sorrow–oh,
then you thrust me forth
and cast me out of Thebes!
Where was your love of kinsmen then?
So now once more–and this time when you find
a city and her sons to welcome me
in gentleness–you wrench my will
with kind words covering your cruelties.
Think! My heart is here, so
how could I rejoice in what you say!
Suppose you had long begged favors
from a friend, but he denied you,
then after, when you had won all,
suppose he offered it–
would you be glad and grateful? No–you bestow on me
a gift of empty words–fair words for speaking;
in the doing, foul. How foul
I'll shortly show to those who listen here.
Not to my home you take me, but to plant my corpse
outside the gate! So Thebes might go scot free
and win a rampart against Athens' spears.
No, no, it will not come–but here in Athens
my avenging soul will abide forever!
My sons? Of Theban soil they will have
dying space as their inheritance,
so much, no more. I am versed, Creon,
in Theban affairs, not you, and the more
since my informants are infallible,

the oracles of Apollo and of his father,
Zeus.
But false words, Creon, and ground to bitterness
you've brought to Athens, and in speaking them
you've won not rescue but disaster
for yourself. I know I shall not move
you to acceptance of these things.
So let me alone. Even as I am, to live here
I shall be content.

CREON

I am amazed! For your ill-omened words
fall on your own head not mine!

OEDIPUS

I am happy in this only—that your
words are powerless to persuade me
or those who listen here.

CREON

Fate-smitten wretch!
Not even time instructs you—
shame only grows with your graying hairs.

OEDIPUS

What a tongue for twisting
all of my words into their opposites!

CREON

Few words I speak, but always to the point.

OEDIPUS

Words to the point!

CREON

Your wits are failing, Oedipus.

OEDIPUS

Go! For myself I speak and for all.
Here must I live, by the will of heaven.
Now take your spies and go!

CREON

All of you be my witnesses—
with curses he has requited the kindness
of his kinsmen. Wait until you are my prisoner.
I'll—

OEDIPUS

I, your prisoner? Never—for these are my allies—

CREON

And even before your capture you will grieve again.

OEDIPUS

You threaten me. What have you done?

CREON

Your daughters—one I have seized, the other
will be taken soon.

OEDIPUS

O my friends—do not forsake me now.
Drive this blasphemer from your country.

CHORUS LEADER

Go and quickly! From the moment of your coming here
you have committed crimes.

CREON

(*To his* GUARDS)
Yes, it's time—willing or unwilling take her off—

ANTIGONE

I am lost! What god, what man can help me.

CHORUS LEADER

(*To* CREON)
And now?

CREON

These are my captives—

OEDIPUS

O rulers of Athens!

CHORUS LEADER

Outrage—

CREON

No, justice—

CHORUS LEADER

Justice!

CREON

I am the guardian—my wards—

OEDIPUS

O Athens, help me!

CHORUS LEADER

(*To* CREON)
What? Let her go! This will mean fighting between us—

(*The* CHORUS LEADER *goes up to* CREON.)

CREON

Keep off—

CHORUS LEADER

Not while you try to take them.

CREON

(*As the* CHORUS LEADER *puts his hand on* CREON'S *arm*)
War with Thebes—if you touch me.

OEDIPUS

I warned you all!

CHORUS LEADER

Take your hands from her—quick!

CREON

Since you are not ruler here–give me no orders.

CHORUS LEADER

Release the girl!

CREON

(*To the* GUARDS)
On your way with her!

CHORUS LEADER

(*Shouting*)
O men of Colonus, come and help! Our city falls to naked violence–

ANTIGONE

My friends, I am dragged away–

OEDIPUS

Where are you, child?

ANTIGONE

They are forcing me to leave you.

OEDIPUS

Your hand.

ANTIGONE

I cannot–I can do nothing–

CREON

(*To* ANTIGONE)
You resist?

OEDIPUS

Lost, now I am lost!

(*Exit* GUARDS *and* ANTIGONE.)

CREON

(*To* OEDIPUS)
These crutches–

ıow no longer will you have them, Oedipus,
:o support your vagrancy.
You abuse us all—your fatherland,
/our friends. Well, I act under their command.
3esides, I am the king. Revile us, but time
vill show your follies—and how wrong
/our frenzied rage,
vhich ever was your bane.

CHORUS LEADER

(*Going up to* CREON)
Stop!

CREON

Drop my arm—

CHORUS LEADER

won't till you release the girl—

CREON

Well, soon will Athens give me a better prize.
'm taking more than these away.

CHORUS LEADER

What will you do?

CREON

Make this man here my prisoner.

CHORUS LEADER

A blasphemy to utter it!

CREON

But it will be done at once.

CHORUS LEADER

No—not if the King of Athens strike you first.

OEDIPUS

That shameless voice again—
You'd lay your hands on me?

CREON

Silence!

OEDIPUS

Dread goddesses—
let me not lose my voice,
only once more to speak—vouchsafe me that—
only once more—call down my curse—my curse
on you, foulest of men.
Blind—you wrench from me
my eyes, my girls! I beg the gods,
oh, and the holy sun, all-seeing of all crimes,
may they visit upon you and upon your kin
to live like me—and then to fall
into an old age like mine!

CREON

Do you hear these babblings, men of Athens?

OEDIPUS

They hear, they see that I defend myself
only with words against your deeds.

CREON

Now I shan't curb my righteous wrath
but singlehanded take him prisoner!

CHORUS LEADER

You dare—

CREON

I do.

CHORUS LEADER

Against this city's sovereignty!

CREON

Yes, though weak and single, I
am strong in my cause.

OEDIPUS

Do you hear him? Zeus be our ally—

CHORUS LEADER

Zeus knows the issue of this outrage.

CREON

Zeus perhaps, not you.

CHORUS LEADER

Infamy!

CREON

Which you will bear—

CHORUS LEADER

O men of Athens, captains of my country,
come quickly. Already Creon's guards cross
our border—

(*Enter* THESEUS *and* GUARDS.)

THESEUS

What is this roar and shouting!
heard you at the sea god's altar—
What furious fear made you break up
he sacrificial rite and rush me here?
Speak—

OEDIPUS

know that voice—my friend,
n outrage I have suffered from this man—

THESEUS

Outrage? Who—

OEDIPUS

Creon has done it—
my only, my two girls—snatched
nd dragged them off.

THESEUS

(*To his* GUARDS)
One of you–you–go quickly
to the altars of Poseidon.
Command all troops, hoplites and horse,
to go posthaste to the place where
the two roads meet. Be there before the girls
pass over the borders. I shan't be mocked–
I shan't be mocked by violence before my guest.
Go as I order you. Quick! This man here–
he'd not escape the flogging he deserves
if I unleashed my anger. Now he shall
be tried and treated by the same code
which he invoked in coming here.
Creon, you shall not leave this land
till you bring back the girls and set
them in my presence here. Your actions now
dishonor me, yourself, your fatherland.
In Athens we honor equity and law.
But you invade our city, defy
our sovereignty, seize what you wish
and carry it away. Did you think that I
or Athens would cringe in cowardice?
Or did you reckon we were slaves or nobodies?
Your city–did it train you up for this?
No–Thebes has no desire to
nourish criminals. Nor would they praise you now,
stealing what is mine–what is the gods'–
and taking prisoner two wretched suppliants!
Do you suppose I would have entered Thebes–
even were my mandate just–in full defiance
of your governors or your king? No!
I, a foreigner, dragging persons
out of your country? No. Thebes
does not deserve dishonor at your hands.
Creon–
wisdom becomes old age–but mounting years
have stripped your wits of judgment. I now
repeat the orders: Bring at once
the maidens here, unless you long to live

my prisoner. You have heard me,
but these are not words only–
they are my certain purpose and my will.

CHORUS LEADER

O stranger, it is shining clear, your forebears
were noble but your deeds are crimes.

CREON

Son of Aegeus, you have accused me falsely.
Never did I suppose that Athens lacked
manhood or counsel. No, no, I've done
what I have done, believing that
no one would be so smitten by this man
that he would take my kinsman here
by force against my will.
And this I know–Athenians would never
welcome a father-killer, and a man of shame,
nor one begetting children from
his incestuous marriage. Yes, and the judges
of your high court of the Areopagus,
were they aware–surely they'd deny
all living space to vagrant malefactors.
In this faith I seized my quarry.
Even so, from his capture I would have refrained
had he not called down upon my family
and my head his bitter curse.
Thus injured, and for simple justice sake,
I've countered him. Oh, I am old,
but my wrath is lusty still. Only
with the dead, anger at injustice dies.
So–do as you wish. I am helpless, but
I shall find means to give you back
what you have given me.

OEDIPUS

O vile and shameless one!
Yes, we are both old. But can you
believe these infamies you mouth
will wound my aging head more than your own?

You–spewing from your mouth murders,
misfortunes, marriages–which I unwillingly
have borne. For so the gods willed it,
harboring against my race a primal hate–
against my race, not me! For you cannot find
within my soul the sin which made me sin
so terribly against myself and mine.
Now tell me: If to my father came
an oracle, as it did come, that he would die
by his son's hand–how am I guilty of that crime,
I who was unborn and unbegotten
when Apollo spoke? But more, if born to misery,
as I was surely born, I fought with my father,
yes, with these hands, and killed him,
but not knowing the man I fought and killed,
how can you indict me for this
unwilling crime?
And of marriage with my mother,
of her–though your own sister–you
shamelessly would have me speak. Well,
I will speak, since your foul tongue has touched
this peak of infamy. My mother, I not knowing,
she not knowing, my children bore to me, her son–
unutterable horror! But this one thing
I know–you, willing and willful, mouth these infamies
against her and me.
Unwillingly I did them then, unwilling I now speak.
No, Creon, you cannot prove me infamous–
either from this wedlock, which everlastingly
you stuff into my ears, or for the killing
of my father. Oh, with what bitterness you
hurl that in my teeth! Answer me one thing only–
if here and now a man should come
to kill Creon–in all his virtue–
what would you do? Ask if he were
your father, or on the instant strike?
I think if you loved life, you would
defend yourself, not ask for proofs
that he was not your parent. I do not think
my father, were he to come alive this day,

would call me guilty! No, not my father—
but *you,* lacking all honesty and
to make your argument, utter the unutterable.
And then you speak of Theseus, flattering
his good name, and praise the excellence
of Athenian laws. You forget this:
No land on earth knows better how to honor
the gods in heaven. But you, while praising
Athens, seize me, an old man and a suppliant,
and my two girls as prisoners to carry off!
O you dread goddesses, come to our aid!
Be our allies and so this man will learn
of Athens and the breed of men
who guard this land.

CHORUS LEADER

My king, he is worthy.
His suffering beyond measure
should be avenged.

THESEUS

We've talked enough. The criminals
act with all speed, and we the innocent
stand by.

CREON

I am in your hands—what will you do?

THESEUS

Lead the way—I will come as your escort.
So—if you have the girls nearby, you
can produce them for me. If not, no matter—
Others at full speed are tracking them.
Your guards will never thank the gods
in Thebes for their escape from me. Lead on
and know: You are the prisoner now.
The captives will capture you. Your trick
won't save you, Creon. You've acted
with such brutal arrogance, perhaps
you have accomplices in Athens

on which you lean. I'll see to that. The city
is not so weak, one man can capture it.
Warnings of others you've received as empty
words. Is that what you think of mine?

CREON

You are the ruler here. I shall not argue.
Only in Thebes I will know how to act.

THESEUS

Threaten—but get on! Oedipus,
you remain here and without fear. Believe
me—unless I die—I shall not rest
till I have brought your daughters here
and put them in your arms.

OEDIPUS

May the gods bless you, Theseus,
for your nobility, and for your jealous care
of me!

(THESEUS, CREON *and* GUARDS *go out.*)

CHORUS

Oh, that I were there
when the enemy wheels
in shock of battle—
bronze-throated Ares cries
in a crash of shields!
The fight may come
by Apollo's temple
or by the shore where the torches flare.
Yes, by Eleusis!
Right where goddesses guard
mysteries for mortals—
we may not speak of them,
for our lips are locked
with a key of gold
which their priests have turned—

there must the enemy fight
close to the border.
For Theseus will give battle,
with war cry of victory
rescue the maidens.

No, they flee past the snowy mountain,
the meadow west of Mount Oea,
on horseback flying,
in chariots racing
one with another.
O eye of my soul,
it seizes upon them—
their capture is certain.
Fierce as the War God
the men of Colonus!
Terrible the might of the king!
Can you hear? Can you see?
Bridles that flash in the sunlight,
knights at full gallop!
Oh, the battle brings honor to Athens,
to Poseidon, dear son of Rhea!

Is it now?
Or soon, soon
thc hour of victory?
Eye of my soul,
you pierce that hour.
I see them—
fighters who fiercely dare,
maidens who fearfully suffer
outrage by their kinsman.
Now they meet
in the skirmish of battle.
O Zeus, bring the end to pass—
ordeal into glory.

But would to God, with a dove's wing
I could climb the sky,

climb to a cloud,
watch the battle and rescue!

O Zeus, Zeus,
Of gods all-ruling, of things all-seeing,
grant us luck in this chase,
with triumphant might
to capture our quarry!
On you I call,
Pallas Athena, holy daughter.
On you, hunter Apollo,
and on your sister Artemis,
smiter of the dappled deer,
I entreat your double aid—
bring now your twofold succor
to us
and to our city.

Stranger, I was a true prophet.
As your watchman, I can see the girls
come toward us with an escort of Theseus' men.

OEDIPUS

Where? What are you saying?

(*Enter* ANTIGONE *and* ISMENE *escorted by* SOLDIERS.)

ANTIGONE

O father, father,
would that the gods would let you see,
with your blind eyes, the noblest of men
who brought us here.

OEDIPUS

Child, you are here!

ANTIGONE

The arms of Theseus and his men
saved us.

OEDIPUS

Come to your father, child,
so I may touch you. I'd lost all hope
of your return–come to me.

(ANTIGONE *and* ISMENE *run to him.*)

ANTIGONE

With all our love and joy!

OEDIPUS

But where are you?

ANTIGONE

We come–

OEDIPUS

(*Embracing them*)
Dear children–

ANTIGONE

All fathers love their own.

OEDIPUS

And my crutches–

ANTIGONE

Misfortune's crutches, father.

OEDIPUS

Oh, now I have my dearest ones.
With you beside me I will never die
in utter wretchedness. Cling to me
and breathe again. What an ordeal
of lonely wretchedness for you! Rest,
and tell me, my daughters, in fewest words
what happened there.

ANTIGONE

Our best and quickest answer is this man
who rescued us. Listen to him, father.

OEDIPUS

My friend, surely you must wonder why I have talked
so much, so long, with these two children–
they seemed forever lost! But I know well
my joy in their return I owe to you,
and to you only, who have rescued them.
I pray the gods do all that I've desired
for you and for this country. Only here
in the whole world do I find holiness
and equity and reverence for the truth.
Consider my words are a thanksgiving–
for what I now hold, you and no other mortal
have bestowed. Now your right hand–let me seize it
and kiss your cheek, if that be lawful.
What am I saying? How could I, born to evil
as I was born, how could I desire
to touch a man who has no stain or sin
upon him? No, I will not take your hand
or suffer you to give it. Only kinsmen
should share these evils. Stay where you are.
I can salute you where you stand.
But, as is right, be still my guard and shield,
as you have been all this day.

THESEUS

It is no wonder joy over your children
bursts from you in a flood of words. Nor strange
that you listened to their story before mine.
I am not eager that what I have done
shine in the telling–only in the doing.
One thing I will say: Of what I swore
that I would execute, in no part have I failed you,
Oedipus. The girls are alive, unharmed.
I brought them to you from the hands
of those who threatened them. But how we won

the battle–why recite that story? You'll
learn of it from these two. As I returned,
a question came to me and I want your counsel.
A slight thing–it has set me wondering.
Slight things neglected sometimes
grow big with meaning.

OEDIPUS

What is it, son of Aegeus?
I cannot guess what you are telling me.

THESEUS

A certain man kneels at Poseidon's altar.
They tell me not a citizen but
your kinsman. I saw him as I left–

OEDIPUS

From what country, and what does he ask the god?

THESEUS

I do not know, except for one thing.
He begs a word with you, on no great matter–

OEDIPUS

What sort of word? No suppliant's prayer is slight.

THESEUS

He asks only to speak with you,
and then safe conduct by the way he came.

OEDIPUS

Who could such a suppliant be?

THESEUS

Think if in Argos you have any kinsman
who might ask this.

OEDIPUS

My friend, say nothing more to me!

THESEUS

What is it?

OEDIPUS

Do not press me to speak.

THESEUS

What can it be? You must speak.

OEDIPUS

Your words have told me—oh, so clearly—
the suppliant's name.

THESEUS

Who on earth? And how could you object?

OEDIPUS

It is my son, O king, the man I hate,
whose words will grieve me more than any man's.

THESEUS

You need not grant, then, what he asks.
Why is mere hearing so impossible?

OEDIPUS

His voice is the most hateful sound
could ever strike a father's ear. No,
do not force me.

THESEUS

Not I—it is the suppliant's prayer
that has compulsion. You must respect the god.

ANTIGONE

O father, I am young to counsel you, but
yield to his wish and to the king's and mine.
Be gracious to Poseidon, whose suppliant he is.
Oh, yield and let my brother come.
Surely he cannot twist your settled purpose—
so what harm in listening? If indeed

he has contrived some evil, it will appear
in open speech. Even imagine all wicked,
impious things were done to you—should you
then give him ill back for evil? He is your son.
Many fathers have had bad sons
with bitter passions, but if rebuked
in gentleness, love alters nature.
O father, turn your mind from present ills.
Look back, look back to the anguish
you endured from your father and your mother.
Oh, then you'll deeply know, I'm sure, I'm sure,
how evil are the end and fruit of anger.
Remember—
when you bereaved your eyes of sight—
in your heart is there not much to think upon?
So yield to us. For surely it is wrong
to keep him waiting if he wishes justice.
You, father, to whom good things
have come but now, should you not know,
and well, how to return such graciousness?

OEDIPUS

Let it be as you wish, Antigone,
though for me, grievous and most harsh
to bear. I ask only of you, my friend,
if he comes here, let no one take me prisoner.

THESEUS

I have no wish, Oedipus,
either to boast, or have you listen
to promises repeated. But, God helping me,
you are free from danger here.

(THESEUS *and* SOLDIERS *go out.*)

CHORUS

Whoever, though mortal, refuses
mortality's measure of years
and lusts for excess of living,

for a measureless count of days,
nourishes surely, I tell you,
deep in his breast dark folly.
For as one day follows another
and endlessly lengthen the years,
afflictions will cluster around him–
but joys, where are they to be found?
It is then that fate bestows
its burden of years without number
till the Angel of Doom–the leveler
of all men one with another–
comes with his march without music
of marriage–or dance, or the lyre.
Silence only and
death as an ending.

Not to be born at all–
by every reckoning that is best–
but born, then swiftly to hasten
back to the land before being;
for when youth fades
with all her folly and her lightsome ways,
oh, then, what toil beyond measure,
what infinite woes break over–of
envy, strife and rebellion,
murder red-handed, and battle–
till at the last, old age,
abhorred, impotent, endowed
with all uncharitableness, appears
with his embrace of woe.

Not I alone but this stranger
is caught in time's storm of affliction.
He stands like a crag in the Northland,
flogged by the storms of winter,
lashed by the sea waves breaking.
All griefs and fate and disaster
from head to toe do confound him.
Griefs from the west and the sundown,

griefs from the east and the dayspring,
griefs from the south and the noontide;
and at last, with darkness enclosing,
doom from the night and the north.

ANTIGONE

Ah, now he comes, our stranger,
but with no escort. Father, he is alone
and weeping as he comes.

(*Enter* POLYNICES.)

POLYNICES

O God!
My father's tragedy before my eyes!
What shall I do? Weep first for him
or for my own disasters? Here with you
I find him exiled upon foreign soil–
these rags, filthy with age and grime,
blighting his body. Head without eyes,
hair blown so wildly in the wind!
And you, sister, so you carry a beggar's wallet
for his food. O foulest of mortals,
I prove myself, coming so late
upon your desperate plight. But I do come
that from my own lips, not another's,
you may learn my own afflictions.
O father–
the God of Pity for all men's deeds–He
shares the throne of Zeus. O father–
will you not let compassion come near you now?
Our past transgression and the sum of them
cannot be altered. But for tomorrow
there lives some hope of remedy
for you, for me. Why are you silent?
Speak, father. Do not turn your face from me!
Must I be dishonored and denied
your answer, dismissed without a word,
not even why you hate me? O children

of Oedipus, O my sisters,
try to move those stern, those sullen lips,
so he may not dishonor the god and me,
dismissing without a word Poseidon's suppliant.

ANTIGONE

Speak, O wretched one, all of your heart,
speak words to waken joy, even harsh words, or piteous,
for, hopefully, they will pierce his silence.

POLYNICES

I will speak–you urge me with such grace.
But first the god I'll make my advocate,
for at Poseidon's altar the king himself
lifted me up and sent me here,
granting me all the rights of conference,
of listening and of speaking, then to go
safely from this land. Safe exodus I would
ask also from you, stranger, from
my sisters, from my father. But now,
why I came here upon this mission I will tell:
Banished I am from fatherland and home,
my brother drove me out. And why? I justly claimed
your sovereignty, indivisibly,
as elder son. But Eteocles, your younger,
thrust me out, winning that victory
not in just courts of law, or trial at arms,
but by flattering he won the town.
I have guessed that the avenging Erinyes
and the curse upon you brought these things to pass,
and what I guess, the oracle confirms. So,
banished, I went to Dorian Argos, where
through my marrying I won confederates–
all of the country's best–the warriors
most honored there. This I did to marshal
an army sevenfold strong of warrior spears.
With them and for his crimes I'll hurl Eteocles
from Thebes or die with honor there.
Now to you, father, I come as suppliant,

I, and all my confederate army,
for now they stand in seven companies
and ring with their spears the Theban plain.
Amphiarus is the first, that great spearman,
first in war, first in the skills of prophecy;
the second, Tydeus, Aetolian Oeneus' son;
the third, Argive-born Eteocles;
the fourth, Hippomedontus—his father, Talaos,
sent him to this war. The fifth, Capaneus,
boasts he'll raze Thebes' towers to the ground
with flaming fire. Sixth, Parthenopoeus
comes to us, who took his name
from the famed warrior maid, his mother.
And then I come, your son—am I your son?
At least offspring of your curse and fate—
I, I lead this fearless army against Thebes,
I and my allies, and we beseech you—
by your dear children and by life itself—
give over your fierce wrath against me,
now as I go to bring just punishment
upon my brother, upon the man who cast
me out and robbed me of my fatherland.
If there be any truth in oracles—
they declare that victory and power
goes with those men to whom you join yourself.
So now I beg you—yes, by the fresh springs
of our homeland, and by our guardian gods—
trust me and yield.
For we are beggars here and strangers,
who live by flattering others, and both bound
by the same fate, while he grows arrogant
in Thebes and fat, and mocks us both.
Only ally your will with mine, I'll rout
our enemies with little time and toil.
Expelling him, I'll bring you home again—
at Thebes establish and restore us both.
Mate but your will and your desire with mine,
then I will shout my triumph! If you deny me,
hardly will I return to Thebes alive.

CHORUS LEADER

Now to this man, Oedipus, whom
Theseus sent, speak what seems good to you
before his going.

OEDIPUS

O guardians of Colonus,
had the lord Theseus not sent him here
to me, he never would have heard my voice.
But since the king judged he should, hear my words,
words which will not delight your heart,
foulest of men, who, when you had my throne
in Thebes–which now your brother holds–
you drove your father forth,
robbed him of country, clothed him with these,
these rags which now you weep to see!
Why? Only that now you walk the same path
of affliction. But I, I will not weep
for these. I will endure them while I live,
but living, hold you my murderer,
for you acquainted me with anguish,
you thrust me out! Because of you
I am a wanderer and a mendicant,
begging my bread each day from other men.
Had I not begotten these, my nurses,
I'd not be here alive. They rescued me,
provide me now my living. They are not women,
they are men who share my toil and travail.
But you? Did I beget you, sons? No! No!
God's eye is on you! Oh, when you unleash
your armies upon Thebes, the assault will fail!
Before you raze the town, you'll fall to earth
stained with a brother's blood and he with yours.
But a short while ago, out of my heart
I called up curses to lay upon your head.
Now I rally them as my allies against you.
So you may learn at last not to dishonor
fathers, though they be blind, but reverence them.
This infamy! How different was the path

my daughters took! So now, these curses will
annul your suppliant's prayer, will annul all
your false claim to sovereignty, if, by ancient
law, Justice still shares the throne of Zeus.
Go, worst of men, for you are fatherless,
I spew you forth. Yes, go and take with you
the curses I invoke, for never will
you conquer with the spear your fatherland,
no, nor return again to Argos, but
with a brother's hand kill and be killed
by him who drove you forth. Then may the hateful
darkness of Hades be your fatherland.
I call on those avenging goddesses
and upon Ares, the great destroyer, who
planted hatred within your heart,
bring all these things to pass.
Now, having heard, go,
and as you go, publish these tidings
to all Thebes, to all of your allies who trust you.
Say to them: This is the inheritance
bequeathed by Oedipus to his sons.

CHORUS LEADER

O Polynices, what an unhappy journey
brought you to this place! Now go, and quickly.

POLYNICES

Yes, a journey to doom for me and
for my comrades. To what road's end
have I led you, my Argive army! Yet now
I must be silent. I cannot speak of this
or yet turn back to Argos. To the road's end
I must go on in silence and to my doom.
O daughters of Oedipus, my sisters,
since you have heard our father and his curse,
if it should be fulfilled,
do not leave my body without honor.
Bury me in Thebes, grant me the last rites.
Now you have praise for all your services to him.
Not less of honor will you have

if you but do these offices for me.

ANTIGONE

Polynices, one thing I beg of you.

POLYNICES

Antigone, dear sister, tell me what you ask.

ANTIGONE

Turn back your army to Argos, Polynices,
as quickly as you can! Do not
destroy Thebes city, your army, and yourself!

POLYNICES

Turn back? That cannot be. For once I showed
my troops a coward's fear, then never
could I lead them back again.

ANTIGONE

Why lead them back ever again?
O brother, why must your madness
break all bounds? What can you win
if you tear down and turn to dust your fatherland?

POLYNICES

Antigone, a shameful thing it is to flee in fear.
I am the elder. My brother would mock me
to the death.

ANTIGONE

Oh, see–oh, see, our father's prophecy
for both your deaths comes true!

POLYNICES

And this he wishes. But I must not yield.

ANTIGONE

O miserable one!
Hearing his words of doom, who will dare
follow you?

POLYNICES

These sorry words I'll not report.
A good general tells his troops
only good news, not bad.

ANTIGONE

O my brother, your mind is fixed–

POLYNICES

And do not hold me back. My father
and the Erinyes make my path ill-omened and accursed.
But it is my path, and I will follow it.
Your own unfolding path, I pray Zeus
make it bright with blessing. Living
you cannot help me, but if I die
grant me my due rites of burial. Now,
let me go. We look our last on one another.

ANTIGONE

Oh, my heart breaks.

POLYNICES

No, do not weep for me.

ANTIGONE

O my brother, who would not
weep for one who goes
to a death foreseen, foretold.

POLYNICES

If it be fated, then I die.

ANTIGONE

Oh, no, no, trust me–

POLYNICES

You cannot argue fate away.

ANTIGONE

If I lose you, then I am lost.

POLYNICES

Antigone, perhaps I die–perhaps I live–the gods decide.
But for you, my sisters, I pray heaven
keep you from evil fate, and
give you all blessings you deserve.

(POLYNICES *goes out*)
(*Rumblings of thunder*)

CHORUS

Once again new evils
dense with disaster
from the blind stranger come,
or is it heaven sending
unfailing doom upon us?
For I know
time is Fate's watchman,
vigilant always–
one day
sinking our fortunes,
the next
lifts us on high.

(*A loud clap of thunder prolonged*)

The sky crashes to earth!

OEDIPUS

My children,
will someone go and bring
most noble Theseus to my side?

ANTIGONE

Father, why do you call him now?

OEDIPUS

Soon
this winged thunder of Zeus
will be my escort to the underworld.
Send for him as quickly as you can.

CHORUS

How vast the sky above us!
Now thunder unspeakable
blasts all about our heads–
these are the bolts from God!
Fear stabs my head
and terror takes my heart.
Again! The heavens burn with flame–
what will the end be?
I am in dread–for
lightning never flashes forth
but it foretells
some mighty circumstance–
fair fortune
or a dread catastrophe.

OEDIPUS

My children, the end of my life,
which God has destined, comes.
No longer may I turn away.

ANTIGONE

You know? This is the sign?

OEDIPUS

I know it well, and beg you
with all speed to bring the king.

CHORUS

Oh! See! Again we are surrounded!
This crash pierces my soul.
Have pity, O God!
If you must doom the earth,
our mother, have pity, have pity on us.
Oh, be gracious–
I looked upon this man,
accursed by heaven,
but save me from his doom!
O Zeus, help us!

OEDIPUS

My children, is he near?
I pray he'll find me alive
and my mind clear.

ANTIGONE

You're thinking of your pledge to him.

OEDIPUS

The gift that time will ripen—
my favor and requital
for all his graciousness.

CHORUS LEADER

Theseus, O my son, come!
Where are you? Are you deep in the sacred valley?
Are you still at the sea god's altar?
Leave off the sacrifice and come
for the stranger's offering,
who finds us worthy—
you, and the city, and our friends beloved—
for his great gift
in grace and recompense to us.
Make all speed, my lord!

(*Enter* THESEUS.)

THESEUS

I hear all of your shouting—the townspeople
and the stranger call to me.
And are these thunderbolts from Zeus? Or are they
storms of hail bursting upon us?
I believe heaven torments us.

OEDIPUS

My lord,
I longed for you and you come. The gods
already have blest your journey here.

THESEUS

O son of Laius,
once more, what new thing has come upon us?

OEDIPUS

The scale of my life now tips toward death,
but first I desire deeply to fulfill
my promises to you and to the city.

THESEUS

Is this the sign, then, of your fated end?

OEDIPUS

The heavens themselves declare it,
the sign ordained long, long ago.

THESEUS

Old man,
what are you saying? Make it quite clear.

OEDIPUS

You hear it again—the thundering
and the bolts hurled from his almighty hand.

THESEUS

I bow to what you say, because I know
these words are oracles.
Tell what my part must be.

OEDIPUS

O son of Aegeus,
I will teach you now
the things ordained for Athens and for you
that are beyond the reach of age or pain.
For soon I shall be led, with no man guiding,
to the place where it is fated I must die.
Neither this place nor region reveal to any man,
and so my grave will guard you, and forever,
better than the might of many shields

or foreign spears.
Let not this mystery move into speech,
though you will learn, you only,
when to that place you walk alone.
This thing I'll never tell
to any townsman, nor to my children,
dearly though I love them. You must shield
the secret always and, when you come
to your life's ending, reveal it
to your next in sovereignty, only to him,
then he to his successor, for all time.
So you will be free from Theban spears
and all the descendants of the dragon's teeth.
For you must know
how with light hearts cities attack each other–
even a neighbor that is governed well–
thinking the gods are blind. No, always the gods–
surely, though late–visit their vengeance
upon man's frenzy and his violence.
You would escape such things–
Oh, why do I talk of things you long have known?
Come let us go to that place–
the god is urgent now and is present here,
we must no longer linger.
My children, this way follow me,
I am your guide as you were mine before.
Come, and do not touch or hold me back;
I, alone, seek out the holy mound
where fate will hide me in the earth.
This way, it is here, it is here! Now Hermes
is my guide and you, Persephone,
queen, goddess of the nether world!
O light, darkness to me, once you were my day,
and now your shining rays for the last time
touch me. Already I am walking
upon the last, brief moment of my life
as Hades shrouds me. O my friends,
O best of strangers, may you be blest,
you and your land, and all your followers.

But when you live in fortune, remember me,
remember my death and me,
so these blessings will endure.
They will endure . . .
(OEDIPUS *goes out.*)

CHORUS

O hidden goddesses—
if you I may entreat with honor,
and you, Lord of the Kingdom of Night,
Aidoneus, Aidoneus, I beseech you!
Let the stranger come without pain
or the doom of violent dying,
to your shrouded world,
to the level lands of the dead ones,
the Stygian home.
For many punishments,
senseless and vain, has he endured.
Lift and renew him in honor,
O God of Righteousness!

O Goddesses
of the world that is under—
and you, monster indomitable
who ward the gateway of many visitors—
so goes the eternal story—
hear me, hear me,
lying before your cave—
unconquered guardian of Hell—
and you, O Death,
child of Earth, child of Tartarus,
I beseech you,
when he reaches the world that is under
give him clear passage
to the plains of the shadowy ones.
O Death, I call upon your name, and I entreat you,
deliver the stranger
to his rest eternal!

(*Enter* MESSENGER.)

MESSENGER

My fellow citizens,
my news I give you first in fewest words—
Oedipus is dead.
But all that happened there
around his death
cannot be quickly told.

CHORUS LEADER

O man of many miseries—so he is gone?

MESSENGER

All mortal part of him
Oedipus has left forever.

CHORUS LEADER

How was his passing? Godlike
and without pain?

MESSENGER

You've guessed what rightly calls for wonder.
How he walked from here you know well,
for you were with us then—how no friend guided him
but he himself was guide to all of us.
When he came near the threshold sheer,
those brazen steps deep-rooted in the earth,
he stood, in one of the many branching paths—
you know the place—close to the hollow cave
where Theseus and Pirithous pledged each other.
He paused there,
halfway between the rock of Thorikos
and the hollow pear tree. Then he sat down
by the marble monument, and loosened from his limbs
the soil-grimed garments that he wore.
His children being there, he asked them for water,
water for washing, and to pour
libations to the goddesses. So the girls went
to the rock nearby

of Demeter, goddess of things growing and green;
quickly performed that bidding—bathed and
dressed him as was meet and orderly
for the rites of death. So content, and
nothing left undone which he had bidden.
Oh, then the air was pierced with sudden sound—
Zeus Chthonios, Zeus of the underworld,
spoke to us in thunder, and the maidens,
frozen with fear, fell upon their knees
before their father, crying,
and as they beat their breasts, moan after moan
burst forth. But Oedipus, when he heard that sound—
so piercing and so sudden—clapped his hands
and cried: My children,
your father dies this day, all that was Oedipus
is gone—and all the burden of your care—
a harsh and heavy burden, that I know,
but one word lightens all:
No man could have given you more of love than I.
Now, without Oedipus, lead and live
the balance of your lives—you must.
Crying, they clung to one another
and sobs shook us all. Then, when these grieving cries
had ceased, and the last moan died on their lips,
into that silence a voice from heaven burst—so that
our hair stiffened. It was
the god calling.
Like many voices blended into one:
You! You! Oedipus, why do we delay
our going? And you too long linger here.
Then Oedipus, when he heard the divine summons,
asked that the king be brought to him,
and then he spoke:
My friend, now for these children's sake,
swear, putting your hands on mine,
and you, my daughters, lay your hands upon the king's,
swear never to forsake them, but to do
all your heart tells you for their good forever.
And noble Theseus, holding back his tears,

promised and gave his oath. When this
was finished, Oedipus turned and laid
blind hands upon his daughters: O my girls, he cried,
now must your hearts be strong. Go,
go nobly from this place. So all forbidden things
you will not see, you will not hear–
only the lord Theseus may stay on
to know the things to be. These words
we all heard from his lips, and as
the girls obeyed, we followed, weeping,
and then turned–turned and looked long–
for Oedipus was not there. We saw only the king,
his hand before his eyes as though a vision,
awful and divine, had blinded him.
First standing, then prostrate
on the earth, as though in one breathing prayer,
he called upon the gods
of heaven and of hell.
But of Oedipus, his fate and passing,
no man knows save Theseus only.
This I know: He did not die
from ocean's storm or heaven's lightning.
Either some guide from heaven came,
or the earth opened
gently to receive him in its arms.
When he was taken
there was no sickness, and no crying,
and no pain.
Of all dyings most wonderful!
Perhaps some man will charge me now
with madness in this message. I do not care.
I tell what I have seen.

CHORUS LEADER

Where are the girls and where their escort now?

MESSENGER

They are nearby. And moaning cries
do show that they are coming here.

ANTIGONE

Aaaah!
O God, now there is nothing!
Nothing for us the unfortunate ones
but to grieve and
to mourn the accursed blood,
to mourn our blood and our father's.
While he lived, we bore ever
his burden of toil.
But now, seeing what we have seen,
suffering what we have suffered,
now at the last we must endure
what we cannot speak.

CHORUS LEADER

What do you mean?

ANTIGONE

My friends, you know, you can guess–

CHORUS LEADER

That he has gone?

ANTIGONE

Yes–it was as he wished.
What other death could he desire?
Neither war on land nor storm at sea
defeated him.
The dark plains took him in,
swept to his secret dying.
Oh, but for me
night like death covers my eyes.
How may I live, Ismene,
or where? Is it in foreign lands
that we shall eat our bread of suffering,
or on far seas go wandering?

ISMENE

I cannot speak, Antigone–
Would God that Hades took me,

so in my misery I too could die,
die with the old man,
die with my father–I cannot live.

CHORUS LEADER

My two good children, we must endure
what heaven gives us.
You have lived blamelessly,
so quench these fires of grief
that torture you.

ANTIGONE

Cruel evils of yesterday
I hold them dear.
Things in no wise tender
were tender then to me,
when I held you in my arms!
O father, O my dear.
Now–and forever–
you have put on dark earth
as a garment,
but even below, even in those depths,
our love will find you out!

CHORUS LEADER

Now it is over–

ANTIGONE

Yes–and as he wished.

CHORUS LEADER

You mean?

ANTIGONE

To die in a strange land,
die upon foreign soil,
oh, now forever he has his bed
in the dark world below–
curtained with darkness
but not unmourned,

oh, not unwept!
Now you have all my wailing tears,
O my father–
I cannot hide my misery.
You, dying in a foreign land,
how can I bless you now
with death's ritual which is due?

ISMENE

My wretched sister–O my beloved,
now we are fatherless, what will
be our fate?

CHORUS LEADER

Dear girls,
since his life's end was blest,
cease, cease your grieving,
for no mortal may escape evil
upon earth.

ANTIGONE

Sister, let us hurry back–

ISMENE

Oh, why?

ANTIGONE

Deep longing seizes me–

ISMENE

For what?

ANTIGONE

To see the ground–

ISMENE

The ground?

ANTIGONE

Our father's grave–

ISMENE

You must not go–

ANTIGONE

Oh, why do you rebuke me?

ISMENE

It is that–

ANTIGONE

Yes, go on–

ISMENE

No mortal saw his end.
He died. There was no burial!

ANTIGONE

But lead me to the place.
Kill me where his bones will lie.

ISMENE

(*Thinking of her own grief and loneliness*)
Oh–miserable, alone, helpless,
where am *I* to live in misery?

CHORUS LEADER

Dear children, give over all these fears.

ANTIGONE

Where can I run away, escape?

CHORUS LEADER

Stay here where you are safe.

ANTIGONE

What are you saying?

CHORUS LEADER

Here no evil thing
will strike you down.

ANTIGONE

I know–

CHORUS LEADER

But you are thinking–

ANTIGONE

Of home! That we should go home–
but how, how?

CHORUS LEADER

You must not try–

ANTIGONE

But my pain and sorrow–

CHORUS LEADER

Before, sorrow came upon you.

ANTIGONE

Then it was helplessness–now
despair!

CHORUS LEADER

Oh, I know–
an ocean of evils you have suffered.

ANTIGONE

Zeus, Zeus, where shall we go?
Fate has killed all my hope!

(*Enter* THESEUS.)

THESEUS

Children,
cease your weeping.
We must not mourn events
which have brought blessings
to this land.
And if we do, the gods

will wreak their vengeance
upon us.

ANTIGONE

O son of Aegeus, we beseech you—

THESEUS

For what are you asking?

ANTIGONE

To see our father's grave.

THESEUS

This is forbidden.

ANTIGONE

O my lord, you are King of Athens.
What are you telling us?

THESEUS

My children, your father forbade me
ever to approach the place
or name that holy grave to any man.
This done, he promised
that ours would be a land
forever free from grief and pain.
Heaven heard these words,
and so did that spirit who guards the oaths of Zeus.

ANTIGONE

This is the will of my father?
It is enough. Then
send us to ancient Thebes,
so we may prevent,
by the will of heaven,
the bloody murder of our brothers.

THESEUS

This I will do, and all else besides
that may bring benefits

to you and to the one
who has departed from us.
With the grace of heaven,
I cannot fail.

CHORUS LEADER

Now cease,
and lift no more your wailing cry,
for in the events
which now have been fulfilled
there lives divine authority.

CURTAIN

ANCHOR BOOKS

DRAMA

THE ANCHOR ANTHOLOGY OF JACOBEAN DRAMA, Vol. I, ed. Harrier, AC5a
THE ANCHOR ANTHOLOGY OF JACOBEAN DRAMA, Vol. II, ed. Harrier, AC5b
AN ANTHOLOGY OF GERMAN EXPRESSIONIST DRAMA: A PRELUDE TO THE ABSURD, Rubiner, *Man in the Center;* Kornfeld, *Epilogue to the Actor;* Goll, *Two Superdramas* and *The Immortal One;* Kaiser, *Man in the Tunnel* and *Alkibiades Saved;* Kokoschka, *Murderer the Woman's Hope* and *Job;* Sorge, *The Beggar;* Sternheim, *The Strong Box;* Hasenclever, *Humanity;* Lauckner, *Cry in the Street;* Brecht, *Baal,* ed. Sokel, A365
BRAND, Henrik Ibsen, trans. Meyer, A215a
THE CLASSIC THEATRE, Vol. I, Six Italian Plays: Machiavelli, *The Mandrake;* Beolco, *Ruzzante Returns from the Wars;* Goldoni, *The Servant of Two Masters* and *Mirandolina;* Gozzi, *The King Stag;* Anon., *The Three Cuckolds,* ed. Bentley, A155a
THE CLASSIC THEATRE, Vol. II, Five German Plays: Goethe, *Egmont;* Schiller, *Don Carlos* and *Mary Stuart;* Kleist, *Penthesilea* and *The Prince of Homburg,* ed. Bentley, A155b
THE CLASSIC THEATRE, Vol. III, Six Spanish Plays: Fernando de Rojas, *La Celestina;* Cervantes, *The Siege of Numantia;* Lope de Vega, *Fuente Ovejuna;* Tirso, *The Trickster of Seville;* Calderón, *Love after Death* and *Life Is a Dream,* ed. Bentley, A155c
THE CLASSIC THEATRE, Vol. IV, Six French Plays: Corneille, *The Cid;* Molière, *The Misanthrope;* Racine, *Phaedra;* Lesage, *Turcaret;* Marivaux, *The False Confession;* Beaumarchais, *Figaro's Marriage,* ed. Bentley, A155d
FIVE COMEDIES OF ARISTOPHANES, A57
FIVE PLAYS OF STRINDBERG, trans. Sprigge, A219
GOETHE'S FAUST, trans. Kaufmann, A328
HEDDA GABLER AND THREE OTHER PLAYS, Henrik Ibsen, trans. Meyer, A215c
THE MODERN THEATRE, Vol. 1: Büchner, *Woyzeck;* Verga, *Cavalleria Rusticana;* Becque, *The Woman of Paris;* Brecht, *The Threepenny Opera;* Giraudoux, *Electra,* ed. Bentley, A48a
THE MODERN THEATRE, Vol. 2: Musset, *Fantasio;* Ostrovsky, *The Diary of a Scoundrel;* Schnitzler, *La Ronde;* Yeats, *Purgatory;* Brecht, *Mother Courage,* ed. Bentley, A48b
THE MODERN THEATRE, Vol. 3: Gogol, *Gamblers;* Labiche and Marc-Michel, *An Italian Straw Hat;* Conrad, *One Day More;* Giraudoux, *Judith;* Anouilh, *Thieves' Carnival,* ed. Bentley, A48c
THE MODERN THEATRE, Vol. 4, From the American Drama: Swerling, Burrows, & Loesser, *Guys and Dolls;* Fitch, *Captain Jinks of the Horse Marines;* Mitchell, *The New York Idea;* Wilder, *Pullman Car Hiawatha;* Saroyan, *The Man with the Heart in the Highlands,* ed. Bentley, A48d
THE MODERN THEATRE, Vol. 5: Büchner, *Danton's Death;* Gogol, *The Marriage;* Ghelderode, *Escurial;* Anouilh, *Medea;* O'Casey, *Cock-a-Doodle Dandy,* ed. Bentley, A48e
THE MODERN THEATRE, Vol. 6: Musset, *Lorenzaccio;* Wedekind, *Spring's Awakening;* Sternheim, *The Underpants;* Beerbohm, *A Social Success;* Brecht, *The Measures Taken,* ed. Bentley, A48f
PEER GYNT, Henrik Ibsen, trans. Meyer, A215d
PIRANDELLO'S ONE-ACT PLAYS, trans. Murray, A404
SIX PLAYS OF PLAUTUS, trans. Casson, A367
SIX PLAYS OF STRINDBERG, trans. Sprigge, A54
THE WAKEFIELD MYSTERY PLAYS, ed. Rose, A371
WHEN WE DEAD AWAKEN AND THREE OTHER PLAYS, Henrik Ibsen, trans. Meyer, A215b

PB 0005737

A 14a

LOT 503-12

469-1067